Yes Changes Everything: Opening the Door to Spiritual Transformation

By John and Donna Avant.
Copyright © 2020 by Life Action Ministries.

ISBN 978-1-934718-74-2

Life Action Ministries
P.O. Box 31
Buchanan, MI 49107
800-321-1538
Info@LifeAction.org
www.LifeAction.org

Editors: Tim Grissom, Kim Adams, Karen Roberts
Designers: Allison Richcreek, Austin Loveing, Emily Crawford

Published by Life Action Ministries.
Printed in the United States of America.

YES
CHANGES EVERYTHING

Opening the Door to
Spiritual Transformation

JOHN & DONNA AVANT

ENDORSEMENTS

I'm thrilled to recommend *Yes Changes Everything*, a new book by my dear friends John and Donna Avant. It's a reminder that you don't need to have life figured out—you just need a willingness to say yes to God. The Avants' story is sure to inspire yours.

Dan T. Cathy
Chairman / CEO
Chick-fil-A

John and Donna Avant have been dear friends for many years, and their lives and ministry are a portrait of what they write about in *Yes Changes Everything*. And indeed, *yes* does change everything. I am thrilled about the work they are doing with *Life Action*, inviting people everywhere to a deeper relationship with the Lord. God has an exciting and productive purpose for every one of us, and the sooner we say yes to Him, the sooner we can begin! This book could be the fresh start you are looking for.

Dr. Crawford W. Loritts, Jr.
Author, Speaker, Radio Host, Senior Pastor
Fellowship Bible Church, Roswell, Georgia

Yes! I first said yes to the Lord at the age of nine, when I gave my heart and life to Jesus. There have been many opportunities to say yes to Him since that day. It is true that God speaks primarily through His written Word, but He also speaks through His indwelling Spirit. Jesus said, "My sheep hear my voice." Have you surrendered and in humble obedience chosen to follow Christ? If you have, this book will help you further develop your ability to hear His voice and then obey.

My husband and I have known John and Donna Avant since our early days in seminary. They have much to offer through personal and ministry experience. *Yes to Jesus* has been their lifestyle. For each of us, the adventure of the abundant life Christ died to give us is just a yes away.

Donna Gaines
Bible Teacher, Author, Pastor's Wife
Bellevue Baptist Church, Cordova, TN

This book is about one of the most powerful and life-changing things a follower of Christ can do: put their YES on the table and let God put it on the map. As D. L. Moody famously said, "The world has yet to see what God can do with one man or woman fully devoted to him." May *Yes Changes Everything* inspire that kind of obedience!

Pastor J. D. Greear
Pastor of The Summit Church
President of the Southern Baptist Convention

Within the past few months, my wife and I have lived out this reality, that **yes changes everything**. When God changes your heart, the rest of your life will change. John and Donna Avant have presented us a book that inspires and challenges us. If you want your willingness to be awakened, read this book. The power and promises of God await you!

Dr. Ronnie Floyd
President / CEO
Southern Baptist Convention Executive Committee

Whether you are a new Christian establishing spiritual roots or a seasoned believer bearing spiritual fruit, the next step in your discipleship starts with one yes to God. With warmth and honesty, John and Donna Avant guide you toward spiritual breakthrough in the overcoming hope that God can transform any situation and every heart. Refreshingly simple, but not simplistic, *Yes Changes Everything* is the perfect starting place for anyone who needs a fresh work of God's enabling grace.

Katie J. McCoy
Assistant Professor of Theology in Women's Studies, Scarborough College at Southwestern Baptist Theological Seminary (TX)

What is holding back the revival of God we long for? Why is the manifest glory of God missing in the church throughout North America? What is God waiting for? The answer is simple although not easy: a simple yes. John and Donna are not theorists. They are first-hand witnesses and instruments of a widespread movement of

God. And they have surrendered their lives to call millions to unite in saying a resounding YES to God. May this book put a fire in your heart and a vision for revival that will never die!

Byron Paulus
Executive Director / CEO
Life Action Ministries

PREFACE

John Avant

For almost a half century, God has used *Life Action* to help people, families, and churches take a "holy pause" and experience His reviving power. When I became president of *Life Action* in 2017, I immediately began to see the kind of deep, life-changing results I had always dreamed of seeing in the people I pastored. I realized that *Life Action* has a unique way of inspiring people to simplify all the myriad issues they face—just hear God and say YES!

At *Life Action*, we want to get this message into the lives of as many people as we can, in every way we can. That's the purpose of this book. Whether you are a new believer, a seasoned Christ-follower, or a seeker, this book is for you. When you are broken by sin or the circumstances of life, or when you have lost the passion for God you once had, or when your relationships are coming apart, or when you feel hopeless, this book is for you. Because the simple truth is, God is real, He loves you, and He will speak to you. And when He does, and you answer with yes, He changes you. That's just what He does. He changes everything. So come with us on this journey into your next YES to God!

ACKNOWLEDGMENTS

John Avant

My wife and I have written this book as a team. God healed our marriage over twenty-five years ago, and since then He uses us best together. Also, one chapter is written by Dan Jarvis, Director of Messaging at *Life Action*. So you'll get a taste of the message of *Yes Changes Everything* from another leader, who lives what he teaches through adoption and global outreach. We are so thankful Dan said yes to being a part of this book.

We would like to express our deepest appreciation to the following:

Meg Groce, for being an assistant and a part of our family for over twenty years.

Aaron Paulus, Communications Director at *Life Action*, for providing invaluable leadership on this project, along with his amazing team: Cristi Fredericks, Kim Adams, Emily Crawford, Allison Richcreek, Nathan Cowles, Carter Warn, Graham Ward, and Wayne Lake.

Troy and Rachel Bowlin, for being a reminder that God changes lives every day.

John and Cindy Cameron, for allowing us to share Jason's story.

Missionaries around the world we are unable to name due to security reasons.

And the following for providing insight, inspiration, and prayers along the way: Billy and Linda Foster, Kristi Nolan, Gary Witherall, and Tricia Kimbrough.

All our many prayer and financial supporters, for allowing us to live out our yes.

DEDICATION

We would like to dedicate this book to every *Life Action* missionary. You choose every day to say yes to Jesus. Lives are being changed daily.

We would also like to dedicate this book to our children and grandchildren and the generations of Avants to come. May you choose to give your wholehearted yes to Christ every day of your life:

> Matt, Christi, William, and Isaac Watson
> Joseph, Amy, Addison, Aubrey, and Judah Daniel
> Trey and Brooke Avant, and baby due in 2020

IN LOVING MEMORY

> Paul Avant, a dad who lived a lifestyle of saying yes.

> Don Duniven, a dad who said yes toward the end of his life and made it count.

CONTENTS

INTRODUCTION

John Avant

Yes.

One of the shortest and simplest words in any language . . . yet loaded with meaning.

"Yes, you're hired."

"Yes, I will marry you!"

"Yes, I'm pregnant!"

At some of the best moments in life—when we complete the challenge, when our team wins, when we get the best news—that one word says all we long to hear.

But then there are other times.

"Yes, it's cancer."

"Yes, I lost my job."

"Yes, Dad's gone."

Yes is indeed one of the most significant words in any language. It is full of possibility and power, expressing deep emotions, opening doors, affirming both fears and joys.

Sometimes, though, *yes* takes on a dimension that is far beyond our humanity—when the Creator of the universe speaks and awaits our response.

Donna and I visited with dear friends recently who are missionaries in an area where the government opposes the message of Christ. As we talked, our friend (who I will call Jeff) told us about a man he and his wife had been sharing with for years. They both felt he was drawing closer to faith, and Jeff said that he had awakened that very morning with this man on his heart and wished that we had time to visit with him.

Just then the doorbell rang. This man we had been speaking about (I'll call him Isaac) had come to visit unexpectedly. Isaac had found out from his doctor that he was sick, and he wanted Jeff and his wife to pray for him. Jeff introduced Donna and me, and a conversation began that led to the defining moment of this man's life.

"I want you all to pray that God will heal me," Isaac said. "I have watched you Christians, and when you pray, God answers you."

"Of course we will pray for you, Isaac," Jeff said. "We have been praying for you for a long time. But you have a greater need than to be healed of this illness. If you believe in my God, who we have told you about, He can heal you forever!"

"I do believe! I have watched your family for years. You are different from everyone else I know. You care for others, not just yourself. You have a power no one else has. Yes, I have decided to believe in your God."

There it was. *Yes.* I was ecstatic.

But Jeff responded wisely. "Isaac, here is your problem. You want my God to take care of you. You have asked us to pray for you before. But I have been to your house and seen many idols there. My God is Jesus, and He is the only true God. Do you believe this?"

"Well, yes, but those idols are part of my family religion. It would be disrespectful to my family not to worship other gods. But I will make Jesus a very important god in our home."

Jeff stood and put an empty chair in the middle of the room. "Isaac, this represents the 'Jesus chair.' No matter what gods you worship, in reality He is the only one who can sit in this chair. Only Jesus. He is here, and He is speaking to you right now. He is calling you to say yes to Him—and only to Him.

"When your car breaks down, you want to put your keys in the Jesus chair for Him to fix it. When you have financial problems, you want to put your wallet in the chair for Him to re-supply it. And now that you are sick, you want to put a medicine bottle in the chair so He will fill it and make you well. But Jesus wants *you. All* of you.

Will you bring all of yourself to the Jesus chair?"

"I want to. But to leave behind all my gods . . ."

"Isaac, I have watched your wife dust off the idols in your home. What kind of god needs to be dusted off? You will have to choose Jesus alone, over all your dusty idols."

Jeff's words to Isaac at that point in the conversation were among the most powerful statements I have ever heard anyone make.

At that moment Isaac's phone rang, and he chose to answer it. The next half hour or so of the conversation was filled with one distraction after another. We could literally feel the war in the spiritual realm going on, the intense battle for the soul of a man.

Finally, all was quiet, and Jeff looked intently at Isaac. "Isaac, what is your decision? The real God, the only God, is calling you right now. Will you say yes?"

Isaac slowly stood up and walked to the chair in the middle of the room. He looked at it for a moment and then sat down. "Yes! I choose Jesus, and only Him."

YOUR CHOICE

Now it's *your* turn to respond. The most important *yes* of your life comes when God speaks to you, and you respond in believing faith. But that *yes* is followed by many more opportunities to respond. Everyone who receives Jesus as Savior becomes His follower and friend.

"I no longer call you servants, because a servant does not know his master's business. Instead, I have called you friends, for everything that I learned from my Father I have made known to you" (John 15:15).

These words tell me that God is *always* speaking to us, telling us what He is doing, calling us to join Him, inviting us to say yes to His love and to His mission. "God wants to speak to us *today,* and every day, through his word. God's word is not simply 'once spoken.' God's word is always 'now speaking.'"[1]

Do you hear Him now? He is not silent. He is not far away. He is calling you. And the most important thing in your life, now and forever, is to hear Him and respond with a resounding YES.

If God is everything the Bible says He is—the Creator who holds the universe together; the living Word; the Savior who rescues you from your sin; the powerful Friend who will sustain, heal, and comfort you; the great God who invites you into His eternal purposes; the coming King who will make all things new—then what could possibly matter more in your life than saying yes to Him?

Are you ready?

QUESTIONS FOR THOUGHT

1. Isaac said to Jeff, "I have watched your family for years. You are different from everyone else I know. You care for others, not just for yourself. You have a power no one else has." Could this statement be made about your life? About your family? Why or why not?

2. Ephesians 1:18-20 says, "I pray that the eyes of your heart may be enlightened in order that you may know the hope to which he has called you, the riches of his glorious inheritance in his holy people, and his incomparably great power for us who believe. That power is the same as the mighty strength he exerted when he raised Christ from the dead and seated him at his right hand in the heavenly realms." Where does Jeff's power come from? What is the purpose of this power? Have you experienced this power in your life?

3. Isaac wanted Jesus to fix his car, heal his body, and supply all his financial needs. But he had not put himself in the Jesus chair. In Matthew 22:37, Jesus says, "Love the Lord your God with all your heart and with all your soul and with all your mind." Have you placed your entire life in the Jesus chair? Take a moment to actually sit in a chair (any chair will do) as a symbol of your decision to follow Him.

4. Jesus explains in John 15:15, "I no longer call you servants, because a servant does not know his master's business. Instead, I have called you friends, for everything that I learned from my Father I have made known to you." What is He saying to you right now?

chapter one

GOD STILL SPEAKS
John Avant

*If you haven't already, it's time to discipline your life so
that you expect to hear God. Hearing from God is normal
in our lives—not normal in impact, but normal in the flow
of our days.*

On February 28, 2018, astronomers announced that they
had "heard" the first stars in the universe.[2] I didn't know stars had
a voice, but apparently they are speaking to us.

Actually, I shouldn't have been surprised, since God told us
long ago, "The heavens **declare** the glory of God; the skies **proclaim**
the work of his hands." "Their **voice** goes out into all the earth, their
words to the ends of the world" (Psalm 19:1, 4).

These scientists had placed sensitive listening devices in the
Australian outback to pick up the faint sounds of a particular kind
of radio wave supposedly produced near the beginning of time
by the first stars. I don't know if they really heard the voice of the
first stars, but I know this: We can hear the voice of the One who
made them.

The voice of the LORD is powerful; the voice of the
LORD is majestic (Psalm 29:4).

The Lord is not slow to speak to us. He invites us to hear His voice: "Call to me and I will answer you and tell you great and unsearchable things you do not know" (Jeremiah 33:3).

Do you want to hear the voice of God?

My five-year-old grandson, William, loves to tell me about the planets. One day he told me that Mercury was "weally, weally hot." Then he told me that Jupiter has a "big wed spot." I asked him what he knew about earth. He said, "Papa John, that's where I live with my mommy and daddy and keep all my stuff!" Then he asked, "What planet do you come from, Papa John?"

I thought to myself, *Sometimes I'm not sure!*

Life on earth gets pretty confusing, which is why it's so important to hear God. He is constant. His voice is clear and unwavering, calling to us even in the darkest moments when we can't see the way forward.

To hear God, we have to be able to filter through a lot of noise. Those astronomers who wanted to hear the first stars had to go someplace where they could escape the noise.

Where will we go to really hear the voice of God?

HEAR GOD SPEAK

Hearing God is characteristic of being a Christian. Jesus said, "My sheep listen to my voice; I know them, and they follow me" (John 10:27). There's no ambiguity; if we know Jesus, we hear Jesus, and we respond to Him.

God rarely speaks the way people speak. For instance, He seldom speaks in an audible voice. In the biblical record, centuries passed with no account of God speaking to anyone audibly. And when He did, it was almost always terrifying. Moses, Isaiah, Mary, Paul, and many others trembled when God spoke to them. God frequently had to say, "Fear not," because He knew that hearing Him could be frightening.

But not anymore.

Through Jesus Christ we can hear the voice of the sovereign God and also the voice of our Savior and Friend. Hearing from God is normal in our lives—not normal in impact, but normal in the flow of our days. We should expect to hear from God.

Jesus told His disciples, "I have much more to say to you, more than you can now bear. But when he, the Spirit of truth, comes, he will guide you into all the truth. He will not speak on his own; he will speak only what he hears" (John 16:12-13). In other words, the Spirit of God lives *within* those who know Him, so of course He speaks to them.

My dad was the greatest man I ever knew. He died suddenly in 2013. He left me with so much—not just love and legacy, but also written words. Dad wrote his own commentary on the red-letter words of the Gospel of John. He wrote it for his family to have when he was gone. He called it *Jesus Speaks*.

As I read Dad's thoughts in his commentary, I understand his greatness better; he was just a simple man who listened to God. "Jesus' words," my dad wrote, "transcend time, and it is just as if He is speaking them now to me . . . and He will be speaking them to every future descendant of my family."[3]

Dad believed that hearing God speak is the key to everything. "As Jesus speaks, I am continuing to run my course. I believe that now or in the future there will be children, grandchildren, descendants, or others that only God knows, who will benefit from what I have learned along the way . . . as I have listened to Jesus speak."[4]

Maybe you are among the "others that only God knows" who will benefit from the wisdom Dad passed on to me—wisdom that reminds me, the most important thing in life is to hear God speak and to say yes.

READ THE BIBLE AS THE VOICE OF GOD

The Bible is called the *Word* of God because it is just that. The Bible is God speaking. Every word of the Bible is "God-breathed" (2 Timothy 3:16). Jesus said, "Heaven and earth will pass away, but my words will never pass away" (Mark 13:31). In the Bible we have words written centuries ago that still speak to us today, and will forever to those who read them.

Do you read the Bible for helpful advice? To learn how to have a better life? To feel better when you feel bad?

Or do you read the Bible to hear God speak?

That distinction is very important. The Bible was not given to us as just a helpful guide to a good life. It was given to us so that we might encounter God and be changed by Him. Reading the Bible with this in mind is thrilling. When you do so, you can expect that God knows exactly what you need to hear and that He will speak directly to you.

Here's an exercise you might try. Take a concordance or an online topical tool to search for what you are dealing with, as if you are asking a question of God. If you are angry, search to see what God says in His Word about anger. If you are tempted, search for the word *temptation*. Read the biblical passages your search reveals. Listen to God speak.

ASK GOD TO CONNECT HIS WORDS AND YOUR EXPERIENCE

Every morning in the shower, I pray something like this: "God, I am too stupid to live this day on my own. Please help me to hear You and to connect what You are saying to my experiences, my decisions, and the people I encounter."

It is astonishing how I hear God and see Him work when

I connect the dots of what He says to what I experience. In 2017, I was the pastor of a church in Knoxville, Tennessee. Donna and I loved that church, and still do, but that was a tough year. We dealt with significant opposition, painful gossip that we could not answer without hurting others, and my own mistakes as a leader.

We had plenty of love and support from the church, but something had changed in my heart. I had dealt with almost every kind of church problem over 35 years as a pastor, but this time it was me who was different. I was constantly sad. I had no idea what to do. My mind told me that there was no reason to feel this way, that I had a wonderful church (with problems like any other), and that I simply needed to love God, love the church, and press forward. But I could not shake the sadness.

One day while reading the Bible as God's Word to me, which I had taught so many others to do, I was struck by how often God's servants went through times of sadness, often for long seasons. Great leaders like Elijah, Jeremiah, David, and Paul found themselves almost unbearably sad, yet God had not abandoned them. He was speaking to them *through* their sadness.

I was drawn especially to the honesty of David: "How long, LORD? Will you forget me forever? How long will you hide your face from me? How long must I wrestle with my thoughts and day after day have sorrow in my heart?" (Psalm 13:1-2).

Then, when David drew from what he knew about God, he began to *expect* Him to speak: "Look on me and answer me, LORD my God" (v. 3). And God *did* speak.

David heard and responded: "I trust in your unfailing love; my heart rejoices in your salvation" (v. 5). Throughout his life, David continued to listen to the voice of the Lord, no matter how he felt. In fact, he acknowledged that God even spoke through those painful feelings. Later, David would write, "The LORD is close to the brokenhearted and saves those who are crushed in spirit" (Psalm 34:18).

As I read these words, I heard God speaking to me.

I was not alone in my sadness. God was about to use my sadness as a vehicle to take me into a new season.

In April of 2017, I spoke at a conference at the Billy Graham Training Center. During the conference, Donna and I went to the altar and surrendered our lives afresh to the One who was speaking to me in my sadness. We were listening to His voice and were ready to say yes.

What we did not know was that leaders from *Life Action* were present and were led, soon after that, to approach me about taking on the role of president.

Could this be the reason behind my sadness? I wondered. *Could this be His voice?*

Then they informed me that it was a missionary position without a salary. We would have to raise our own financial support.

That wasn't in our plans.

Once again I returned to the Word to hear God speak. I began to hear His call, inviting Donna and me to uproot and join Him in this new journey. We said yes to Him and left the pastorate, which had been our life for so many years. But I struggled with the fear of having no salary.

A few weeks later, I hiked up into the Smoky Mountains to a place I call "my oasis," where three waterfalls converge. I sat there alone with God all day and listened to Him speak from His Word and through His Spirit.

I read in the short book of 3 John, where John praised his wealthy friend Gaius for helping missionaries who had come his way, even though he didn't know them. "Dear friend, you are faithful in what you are doing for the brothers and sisters, even though they are strangers to you. . . . It was for the sake of the Name that they went out" (3 John 5-7). Suddenly, I could hear the voice of the Lord, as if He were shouting to me over the roar of the waterfalls: "If you will trust Me, I will send even strangers to help you."

I went home and told Donna. Together we began watching for God to fulfill His Word. We didn't have to wait long.

About a month later, a man called and asked to take me to lunch. He and his wife had recently come to the Lord. They had been coming for a short time to the church where I was pastoring, but we had not had the opportunity to talk. I knew nothing about him, but as we talked, I was amazed at how God had healed his marriage and delivered him and his wife from alcohol and drugs—all without any human counsel. They just read the Bible, believed God was speaking, and did what He said.

Donna and I began to disciple this couple, and to this day they are very close friends of ours. During that initial time of discipling, they asked to support our ministry financially. In fact, they became among our largest supporters—strangers, now friends, sent from God to help us do what God had asked us to do. Through them we learned all over again how God speaks, and how wonderful it is to live by faith, hear His voice, and just say yes.

Asking God to daily connect His words to your experience will lead you to a life you don't want to miss.

LIVE LISTENING

If you haven't already, it's time to discipline your life so that you expect to hear God. As a follower of Jesus, you never go anywhere He is not. His Spirit lives in you. You have the daily opportunity of being filled with His Holy Spirit (Ephesians 5:18). But you can still ignore Him or pay more attention to all the other noise until His voice is hard to hear.

I challenge you to take the next forty days and ask God several times each day to help you hear His voice. Forty days is an important time segment in the Bible, and anything you do consistently for forty days is likely to become a habit in your life.

No discipline will matter more to you than hearing God speak, so make it specific and regular. Join the prophet Habakkuk, who took hearing from God so seriously that he said, "I will stand at my watch and station myself on the ramparts; I will look to see what he will say to me" (Habakkuk 2:1).

In taking this step, you will also change your prayer life from tending toward a more regimented and maybe ritualistic time, into the biblical practice of praying "continually" (1 Thessalonians 5:17). You can literally "breathe" prayers while you are carrying out your normal, daily activities. And don't be afraid to pray with others as the opportunities come to you, believing that prayer with them is also a normal part of the flow of life where God is speaking to you all the time.

Pray with your family members, too, and not just at meals or bedtime. Pray when someone is scared, when they are sad, when something wonderful has happened, when there is a decision to be made . . . Just pray. Talk to God briefly, and listen, and watch what happens around you.

I love watching people and asking God about them. On my own I am selfish and often ignore people. But if I walk in the Spirit and listen to God, I have all kinds of adventures.

I love to talk to and pray with servers at restaurants. I ask God to speak to me about them. I've lost count of the number of servers I have seen come to the Lord this way or become my friends. It's so easy to do, and often God shouts to us in joy as we get to join Him in someone's transformation.

In 2001, I had the difficult privilege of being a chaplain at Ground Zero after September 11. I stood on that burning mound and prayed as dead bodies were discovered. Years later, when Donna and I visited the memorial there, we saw an usher standing next to an exhibit. I asked the Lord about her. I sensed that I should ask her what all this meant to her.

When I did, she looked surprised and said, "I was on the

71st floor of the South Tower when the plane hit. I survived when so many died. And even though I work here, almost no one ever thinks to ask why. I work here because I almost died here."

For a half hour we talked and shared. Then I asked if I could pray for her. I said, "When I was here before, I prayed over people who were dead. Now I can pray over someone who is alive." As I prayed, others heard and stopped and prayed with us. It was a holy moment.

I don't want to miss any of these times. And I won't if I listen to God. Neither will you.

Don't worry too much about messing up. Of course you will misunderstand God from time to time. But He won't be angry at you when you get it wrong. He will use your mistakes to help you know Him better.

As you journey through life hearing God speak, be sure that you listen to the God who *is*, not the God who is *not*. He is not a god of your own making. Even though He will sometimes rebuke and convict you, He is not a god of religion who is out to get you. Neither is He a god of false theology who will shower you with anything you want.

He is **God**. **The** God. The God of the Bible. The **only** God.

Never forget the essential nature of this God: "God is love" (1 John 4:8). When He speaks to you, it is *always* in love, because that is who He is. He cannot speak otherwise, or He would speak contrary to His own nature. No matter what anyone has told you about God, what you have thought about Him, or what experiences you've had that made you question Him, none of those things change the fact that God is love—and everything He says pours out infinite love.

In 2016, I watched on the news as Andrea Diaz received a cochlear implant. For the first time in her life, she would be able to hear. As the doctor turned it on, all she could hear was noise. But then, as it was adjusted, she began to hear. She could hear!

At that moment her boyfriend, who had accompanied her to the doctor, got on one knee next to her. He said, "I love you, Baby. I wanted to make one of the first things you hear from me be asking you to marry me."

But you don't have to be hearing impaired to experience this joy. In Lamentations 3:22-23, God speaks an eternal truth: "Because of the LORD's great love we are not consumed, for his compassions never fail. They are new every morning."

Every day, according to His own Word, the King of glory comes to you and says, "I love you! I love you with a steadfast love. I love you with mercy that never ends. Will you be Mine this day?"

You and I have the great joy of hearing Him, and then we have the privilege of giving Him an answer. How we do that is what the next chapter is all about.

QUESTIONS FOR THOUGHT

1. John 10:27 says, "My sheep listen to my voice; I know them, and they follow me." Are you hearing God? Are you following Christ in every area of your life? Is there a specific area the Lord has spoken to you about where you are refusing to walk in obedience to Him? If so, you will have trouble hearing Him. Choose right now to agree with God about what He has shown you, and walk with Him into obedience.

2. Henry Blackaby says, "Unbelief can render a person stone deaf to God's voice."[5] Do you believe God is who He says He is? How has He revealed Himself to you?

3. How often do you read God's Word? When you read it, are you reading it as a helpful guide to a good life, or are

you reading God's Word to encounter Him, hear Him, and be changed?

4. Take the forty-day challenge and begin your day with a prayer similar to this: "God, I am too stupid to live this day on my own. Please help me to hear You and to connect what You are saying to my experiences, my decisions, and the people I encounter today." Write down what happens in your day after praying this way.

5. As God speaks, He reveals His character to us. Since God is love, He always speaks to us in love! Read the following verses out loud. What is God saying to you?

   • "The LORD your God is with you, the Mighty Warrior who saves. He will take great delight in you; in his love he will no longer rebuke you, but will rejoice over you with singing" (Zephaniah 3:17).

   • "Because of the LORD's great love we are not consumed, for his compassions never fail. They are new every morning; great is your faithfulness" (Lamentations 3:22-23).

   • "This is how God showed his love among us: He sent his one and only Son into the world that we might live through him. This is love: not that we loved God, but that he loved us and sent his Son as an atoning sacrifice for our sins" (1 John 4:9-10).

chapter two

WILL YOU SAY YES?

John Avant

God speaks, but He isn't really interested in a monologue.
He created us for relationship with Him. That means, when
He speaks, He awaits our response. He awaits our yes.

For a few years, Donna and I thought our grandchildren didn't have a sin nature. But time has corrected that perception. Our four-year-old granddaughter, Addy, is an incredibly sweet girl. But one night she decided she wasn't interested in obeying her daddy when he called her to come downstairs.

"No!" she said.

"Excuse me?"

"No!" she shouted again.

Her daddy was up the stairs and in her room in no time. "What did you just say to me?"

"No-ah," she replied. "I said *Noah*—like in the Bible!"

Donna and I laughed out loud over her savvy attempt at avoiding correction from her dad. But it's really not funny when someone says no to God, our heavenly Father, and tries to excuse a sin. And for most of us, this is fairly regular behavior. But it doesn't have to be. And we don't want it to be. Because God is who He says He is, the single most important thing in life is saying yes to Him when He speaks!

Jesus said to His friend Martha, "I am the resurrection and the life. The one who believes in me will live, even though they die; and whoever lives by believing in me will never die. Do you believe this?" (John 11:25-26).

Can you imagine anyone, at any point in her life, asking Martha anything that mattered more than Jesus' question? And her answer? "Yes, Lord, . . . I believe that you are the Messiah, the Son of God" (v. 27).

God had spoken to her. She responded. Her answer was yes. From that point on, her life would be transformed.

The same opportunity is yours!

ENTER INTO THE RELATIONSHIP

God speaks, but He isn't interested in a monologue. He created us for relationship with Him. That means, when He speaks, He awaits our response. He awaits our *yes.*

God intends the life of the believer to be characterized by prayer—a life of talking with God. This is what Paul meant when he said to "pray continually" (1 Thessalonians 5:17).

That verse used to seem so daunting to me, especially as a young believer. "I don't pray enough," I used to think. "I need a longer quiet time!" An extended quiet time wouldn't be a bad thing, but it's not really what a life of prayer is. In fact, notice what "pray continually" is surrounded by: "**Rejoice** always, pray continually, **give thanks** in all circumstances" (vv. 16-18). Those instructions go far beyond what happens during a quiet time.

The passage as a whole is about an active life of seeking to hear God and saying yes to His call to bless other believers and those who don't yet believe: "Always strive to do what is good for each other and for everyone else" (v. 15).

God's words are calling us, as they called the Thessalonians, to an intimate relationship with Him. When He speaks to us, and we hear and say yes, our lives are transformed, and the lives of those around us are transformed as we spread the joy!

I first began to get a glimpse of what God intended life with Him to be like when I was in fourth grade. My family had moved to Ohio, and I was lonely and unhappy, struggling to make new friends. But I had a little dog, a Boston terrier named Ruffles, that I loved desperately. One day, Ruffles got loose in the apple orchard behind our house, and she was gone. Days went by with no sign of her, and I was devastated. My dad came to my bedside one night and suggested that we ask God to help us find Ruffles. So we did.

The next day at school, I heard the boy beside me talking to another boy about his new dog. He had found him wandering the neighborhood and adopted him. He began to describe a little black and white dog. Now, this boy lived miles from me, but suddenly I just knew that God had answered my prayer. I did not even know the Lord yet, but He knew me! So I jumped up and yelled, "That's my dog! You've got my dog!" And I ran out the door to the principal's office.

Once the principal of the school had called my parents and gotten everything calmed down, we found out that my little dog had wandered miles through the woods into another neighborhood and right to the house of the boy who sat next to me in school!

A seed was planted in my heart that day. God cared. God heard. God invited me to talk to Him. And when I said yes, He did amazing things.

In the years that followed, I would think about that day many times and wonder about a God who cared that much about a little boy and his dog. And the wonder has stayed with me all these years, from the saving of my soul to the relationship He allows me to have with Him daily.

What might He do next? What life might He change? What family might He reconcile? What church might He revive? Might He even awaken a nation?

I want to find out!

When God speaks to you, He is seeking your yes. The Bible records twenty-three times when Jesus called people to follow Him. Sometimes it was exciting—"Come, follow me, . . . and I will send you out to fish for people" (Matthew 4:19); sometimes it was hard—"Whoever wants to be my disciple must deny themselves and take up their cross and follow me" (16:24); sometimes it defied human logic—"Follow me, and let the dead bury their own dead" (8:22). But *yes* was always the right answer.

Some people said yes. Peter and Andrew immediately left their nets and followed Jesus (4:20). Some people said no. The rich young ruler said no and "went away sad" when Jesus called him to leave his possessions behind and follow Him (19:22). You will have to choose as well, because He is also calling you.

THE SIX RESPONSES

When I became president of *Life Action*, I joined a ministry that had been responding to the "Follow Me" call of Jesus for years. For nearly half a century, *Life Action* had helped individuals, families, and churches to hear God, say yes, and experience a revived, renewed life. To this day, our mission is "to inspire your next yes to God."

I had never experienced a culture as healthy as what I found at *Life Action*. It was certainly not perfect, but it was clear to me that there was something distinct and wonderful about these missionaries I began to serve and serve alongside. As I dug into what made this ministry unique and what had filled it with such long-term health and spiritual fruit, I kept hearing about something they called the six responses. *What were they?* I wondered.

Life Action has seen thousands if not millions of lives changed, marriages saved, and churches healed by the power of

God. And each time, the people involved said yes to God in one or more of these significant ways. The more I have watched this work and the more I have studied these responses in the Word of God, the more convinced I have become of an exciting truth: **These six responses are how we follow Jesus.**

These responses include both the *way* we say yes to God and the *destination* we reach when we do. Because these responses are the will of God for us, we don't have to "try harder to be a good Christian" or do something impressive for God. He Himself will give us the strength to respond in these ways when we simply say yes to Him. "It is God who works in you to will and to act in order to fulfill his good purpose" (Philippians 2:13).

This truth is incredibly liberating; God is *pleased* to do this in us. He *wants* us to have this empowerment. But we can't go there on our own. We only go *with* Him.

God speaks. He calls us to follow Him. So let's look at these six responses.

1. RESPOND IN HUMILITY

Personally, I am drawn to self-promotion, self-defense, selfish pleasures, and selfish dreams. Before leading *Life Action*, I pastored three large churches. When I entered a room, everyone knew my name. Donna was the pastor's wife. Her identity developed around that. People knew her name as well.

When I left the pastorate, our identities changed. I preach more than I ever did, but my identity is different. Now when I go into a church, often no one recognizes me. The pastor has to explain to the people who I am. I am much more anonymous than I used to be.

Donna and I knew this change would happen. God had even spoken to us about it as we talked with Him about coming to *Life Action*. We sensed Him saying to us, "Will you decrease so I can increase? Will you let your name matter less so that My name can matter more?" That self-centered pull is still there for me, and I must battle it in the spiritual realm. How am I to respond? "Humble yourselves before the Lord, and he will exalt you" (James 4:10 ESV).

I don't know about you, but when I see an amazing, life-giving promise from God such as this one calling me to respond to Him, it motivates me. I have learned through many years of wonderful experiences that God, who owes us nothing, nevertheless makes astonishing promises to us. And He keeps them. I have seen this truth so many times that I have no doubt about it anymore.

Interestingly, the word *humble* is the opposite of *exalt* in this verse. The verb *humble* means "to make oneself lower." So if you will make yourself lower, God will bring you higher in exactly the way He knows is best, and at exactly the right time. I can't tell you how encouraging that is to me.

God has simplified the "how" of humility by demonstrating it. Consider Jesus, as He powerfully demonstrates humility.

> The King of the universe stood from the table—the last table He would eat at before His death—and made His way to an unused towel and basin. As His disciples watched Him, wondering what He was doing, He must have felt His human heart breaking. After three years with Him, his best friends still did not get it.
>
> Every foot in that room was unwashed.
>
> And this was unacceptable as they prepared to eat the Passover meal. In fact, it was unacceptable at any time in those days. The streets of that time had a gutter in the middle that functioned as an open sewer. Everyone walked around wearing open-toed sandals. Their feet were literally covered in sewage dust. Disease-laden bacteria colonized on their feet. They

didn't understand it, but they knew that if you didn't have your feet washed, disease came to your home.

So everyone who could had a servant—the lowest of the low, the humblest of the humble—who would wash their feet.

And now, the Son of God knelt down, and with hands that made the stars, with hands that made these feet, with soon-to-be nail-pierced hands, He washed. He got in between each toe and literally washed the sewage away.

And they were stunned. Yet no one else volunteered. No one else helped. No one else understood. Finally, Jesus told them, "Now that I, your Lord and Teacher, have washed your feet, you also should wash one another's feet. I have set you an example that you should do as I have done for you" (John 13:14-15).

Jesus' example gives us the *how* of James 4:10. What happens when we say yes is truly amazing to me. If you humble yourself, the King of the universe will *exalt* you. He will exalt *you*!

Both words, *you* and *exalt*, are stunning. The word *exalt* can mean "to raise to dignity, honor and happiness."[6] It is also the word used of Jesus Himself in Acts 2:33, referring to His being "**exalted** to the right hand of God."

And then there's that word *you*. It's hard to fathom that God puts the word *exalt* anywhere near me, but He does.

His love is unfathomable, undeniable, and incomparable. So, though I don't know what this exalting will look like or when He will do it—and I'm pretty sure it won't primarily be about the things of this world that soon fade away—I want in on it. He keeps His promises, and this is a thrilling one.

Humility is a better path to my deep-rooted desires than anything I can achieve on my own or that the world can offer me. But far more importantly, because I believe Him, I want to respond to Him and to others in humility.

Humility is not complicated. We don't have to "feel" humble or take a course on being humble. We can just go serve others the way Jesus did. Do what others won't. Love people in simple ways. Make yourself lower, and He will use you in His higher purposes for your life.

2. RESPOND IN HONESTY

Throughout history, religion in its various forms has sparked torture, war, disunity, broken family relationships, anger, pride, and countless hurts, anywhere and everywhere. It sends people to hell while they strive for what they can never achieve on their own—right relationship with God. Religion doesn't just show its ugly face in these large-scale ways; it also creeps into our lives and our churches in seemingly innocent and innocuous ways.

One example is the lack of honesty—some call it *transparency* or *authenticity*—in many believers and churches. Think about your own life. Is it difficult for you to be open with God about your struggles, your doubts, your sins? Are you afraid of His judgment?

Now think about your church. Is it a place where you can openly share those things with trustworthy friends? Or is it a place where you feel the need to create a façade so that others don't think badly of you?

Unfortunately, the latter is often the case in churches, and the exit of a generation from organized religion and its practices demonstrates it. The Barna Group and others have presented ample research showing that a lack of honesty and authenticity is a major reason millennials have left church. They have watched those of us in it and don't find us "real."

The Barna Group found that "two-thirds of Millennials . . . believe that American churchgoers are a lot or somewhat hypocritical (66%). To a generation that prides itself on the ability to smell a fake at ten paces, hypocrisy is a worrisome indictment."[7]

God wants us to be honest and authentic. "Trust in him at all times, you people; pour out your hearts to him, for God is our refuge" (Psalm 62:8). When we pour out our hearts to God together, we experience the truth that He is our refuge.

Life Action sends teams into churches to help them take a "holy pause" and refocus on hearing God. Most of the missionaries we send out came to *Life Action* because *Life Action* first came to them. Their lives were changed through the revival message, and they want to pass the message on. They come to serve, having already embraced honesty and transparency themselves. When they share in churches, they talk openly, when the opportunity calls for it, about their abortion, or their affair, or their anger, or other failings.

Donna and I have joined them in their honesty. We share everywhere we go about the brokenness of our marriage years ago and how God healed us and took us from a place where we hid those problems to a place where we "pour them out" to God and others. Often we see incredible breakthroughs in the lives of individuals and churches. Our honesty establishes an environment of transparency, and others begin to open up and find healing.

The apostle Paul modeled this approach for us throughout his life. He admitted that he often did the things he did not want to do and did not do the things he wanted to do. In his first letter to the Corinthians, Paul tells how much better it is just to be real, not to try to be someone we are not or more than we are:

> Brothers and sisters, think of what you were when you were called. Not many of you were wise by human standards; not many were influential; not many were of noble birth. But God chose the foolish

things of the world to shame the wise; God chose
the weak things of the world to shame the strong.
God chose the lowly things of this world and the
despised things—and the things that are not—to
nullify the things that are, so that no one may boast
before him (1 Corinthians 1:26-29).

If God uses the lowest and weakest in the greatest ways, why
try to be something more than we are? If we do, we will actually
miss the life God has for us.

Responding honestly to God and others is scary at first.
And it can be risky. You may get burned by people who still live in
their own hypocrisy. But it's costlier to be phony, isn't it? So why
not take the risk?

Start by honestly pouring out your heart to God every
day. Tell Him all your doubts and fears. He will listen. And read
the psalms regularly. Sometimes they are so honest they sound
almost blasphemous: "Awake, Lord! Why do you sleep? Rouse
yourself! Do not reject us forever" (Psalm 44:23).

That's bold honesty. But that's the way the psalmist felt,
and he didn't hide it from God. Why should you? God knows
your heart. So, pour it out. Then He can speak back to you in
honesty and guide you to His truth.

Next, take the risk of being honest and transparent with
another person. You may be surprised at how much that person
needs it too. Let this practice become your new normal.

Saying yes to God by being honest with Him and others
will liberate you, enabling you to see God work on who you really
are and who you can become.

3. RESPOND IN REPENTANCE

Repentance is a word that has gotten a bad rap. Not too
many people, particularly those who don't know the Lord, have a

good impression of this word. That's partly the fault of those who have claimed to speak for Jesus while shouting in vitriol at those who have never known the love of a Savior, "Repent!" It's a shame that this word is viewed as bad news, because it's one of the greatest "good news" words of all time.

The word in the New Testament carries the basic meaning of changing one's mind, but the word is never used in the New Testament with *only* that meaning. It's an active word that always means to "turn a different direction." When you repent, your heart is broken over the direction you have been going, so you respond to God by asking for His Spirit to turn you in a different direction. And when you do that, great things begin to happen in you spiritually. God's good way is better than our bad ones. So why would it ever be bad news to repent? Who wants to be going in a bad direction or toward a bad destination?

God tells us clearly what His new direction will be like: "Repent, then, and turn to God, so that your sins may be wiped out, that times of refreshing may come from the Lord" (Acts 3:19).

How wonderful is that? When we repent, our shame and guilt go away, in God's eyes and in our own heart. And then the refreshing comes. He washes over us like a cool mountain stream in the heat of summer. He quenches our thirst. He restores our soul.

Let's just admit, we are often a mess. Let's *change our mind* about excusing our sin and, in the strength of God's Spirit, *turn toward His way*. And when we mess up, as we will, let's get up and repent again.

In 1995, Donna and I had the privilege of pastoring Coggin Avenue Baptist Church, where what has come to be known as the Brownwood Revival began. God moved in power in a small Texas town and on the campus of Howard Payne University. (I wrote about this experience in the book *Revival Revived*.) The movement spread to over a hundred college campuses and many churches across America and beyond. In essence it was a revival of repentance. People of all ages changed their minds and, by the power of God's Spirit, turned His direction.

Twenty-five years after the Brownwood Revival, many of the students God used to start it are now missionaries. They have scattered to the ends of the earth. One of those is Jeff, the missionary in the story told in the Introduction to this book. He, his family, and many others around the world are now part of an awakening that has seen more Muslims come to Christ in 15 years than in the previous 1500.

I urge you to run *toward* the good news of repentance, not away from it. If God is speaking to you about your sin, respond to Him. Let the refreshing begin.

4. RESPOND IN FORGIVENESS

Part of the refreshing that comes from repentance is that we are forgiven. "If we confess our sins, he is faithful and just and will forgive us our sins and purify us from all unrighteousness" (1 John 1:9).

God forgives *all* your sins. So why would you continue to live in the shame of your sin? Stop *feeling* and start *believing*. Respond to God's forgiveness by thanking Him every day that He has forgiven you, and live in that beautiful freedom.

But the coin of forgiveness has another side. It does not end with your own freedom. You need to offer the same freedom to others. "Bear with each other and forgive one another if any of you has a grievance against someone. Forgive as the Lord forgave you" (Colossians 3:13). That's pretty clear; there's no place for unforgiveness in your life. You must share with others the forgiveness given to you.

But I've been wronged! It's not fair. It hurts so much. Someone needs to pay!

I've felt all that. Sometimes I still do. But I know what to do with it. I stop and remember how much I have been forgiven. In fact, when someone is critical of me or slanders me, I have learned to stop and remind myself that I am worse than they think I am. It doesn't matter if they are right or wrong about the particular complaint they have about me. What if they knew everything about my thoughts, words, and actions? They would *really* have cause to dislike me then!

Well, God *does* know. And He has forgiven me. So what reason do I have not to forgive as well? Unforgiveness in my life hurts no one but me. And the bitterness that comes from unforgiveness is a poison that I drink myself in hopes that it will kill someone else!

If it is difficult for you to forgive, read the Old Testament story of Joseph. This poor guy was sold into slavery by his own brothers, falsely accused of attempted rape, imprisoned, and a whole lot more. Yet all the while, God was working for Joseph's good and His glory.

Responding in forgiveness requires faith, doesn't it? Can you believe that even when someone sins against you, God is big enough to use it for good? See how Joseph chose to respond. When he finally had a chance for revenge against his brothers—when he had power over their very lives—he said:

> "You intended to harm me, but God intended it for good to accomplish what is now being done, the saving of many lives. So then, don't be afraid. I will provide for you and your children." And he reassured them and spoke kindly to them (Genesis 50:20-21).

The matter of forgiveness is among the most common and invasive ones for most people in churches where *Life Action* teams minister. Everyone is wounded. Everyone needs healing. Everyone needs forgiveness . . . and everyone needs to forgive. When we see it happen, oh, the beauty of it! Families are reconciled. Friendships are restored. The power of the gospel is unleashed.

So trust God and rejoice. No matter what anyone has done to you, He is right there with you, working it out for good. You can, by His Spirit, forgive and release your anger and hurt toward others—and the freedom of forgiveness begins.

5. RESPOND IN OBEDIENCE

This one is pretty simple: Hear God . . . Say yes . . . Do what He says.

"If you **love** me, keep my commandments" (John 14:15).

We are not expected to obey Jesus out of duty. We don't obey Him in order to become better people. And we don't obey Him because it's the law. *We obey Him because of love.*

This distinction is important because any other so-called "obedience" is not the gospel. It's an empty response, and that's not what we are talking about here.

Here is the simple way it works: God speaks. It starts with Him, not us. He initiates. He loves.

And we respond. We say either yes or no. *No* drives us deeper into self. *Yes* drives us deeper into Him—and into love. Because He *is* love (1 John 4:8). And every time we say yes to God, we want to do it again next time. Obedience becomes easier because we love God so much that we don't want to disappoint or miss Him.

When I was a child, I felt that way about my wonderful dad. I feared his discipline if I disobeyed, but I feared his disappointment more, because I knew how much he loved me.

God loves me infinitely more, as He does you. I can't work my way into obedience. But I can love my way there.

Now, I said this is simple. But that doesn't mean it's easy. There is a battle raging for your *yes*. There is an enemy who wants your *yes*, too. And he puts on a good show. He offers you very attractive alternatives to say yes to. Attractive at least for a while—until they begin to addict and destroy you.

The only way to fight this enemy is to develop an overwhelming view of God that captivates your life and heart and that overwhelms the other options. In other words, **you must become**

more astonished by God than by anything else in the world.

Perhaps the best picture of the God-astonished life in the Bible is found in Isaiah 6. It's 740 B.C., the year that King Uzziah died. He had wasted the latter years of his life and died in disgrace, leaving a confused kingdom. Most ran to their own ways; but one man, Isaiah, ran to the true King.

Isaiah saw amazing things—magnificent and terrifying angelic creatures, smoke and shaking, while the train of the great King's robe filled the temple. (Think two football fields of a flowing robe.) This vision mattered more to him than it does to us today because in ancient days, when one king conquered another king, he would cut off the train of that king's robe and sew it on his own. The longer the train, the greater the conqueror. This King conquered everything!

Isaiah became overwhelmed by his own sin. In verse 5 he shouted, "Woe to me!" *Woe* is a common Jewish word, still in use today as *Oy!* Rabbi Benjamin Blech says, "Within it resides all the pain of the past, the discomfort of the present, and the fear of the future."[8]

Isaiah felt all of that woe as an angel came toward him with a burning coal. Imagine his fear. He's about to be burned alive! But the angel said, "See, this has touched your lips; your guilt is taken away and your sin atoned for" (v. 7).

Do you see what happened in this story? Are the six responses coming alive to you through it? Isaiah first ran to God in *humility* and *honesty*. He met God and experienced *repentance* and *forgiveness*. He was absolutely astonished by God to the point that nothing else mattered except his *obedience*. And then he was ready to put God's *kingdom first* in his life.

Isaiah heard the voice of the Lord! And the Lord, the great triune King, wondered aloud, "Whom shall I send? And who will go for us?" (v. 8). Isaiah lifted his hand in an obedient and enthusiastic YES and shouted, "Me! Let it be me!"

That's how obedience works for us too. We must have a vision of a God so big, so wonderful, so powerful, so astonishing, that we obey Him no matter what. It would seem silly to do otherwise, to give our yes to anyone or anything else.

6. RESPOND BY SEEKING HIS KINGDOM FIRST

"Seek first [God's] kingdom and his righteousness, and all these things will be given to you as well" (Matthew 6:33). Seeking the kingdom of God is one of the most important teachings in the Bible. Jesus talked about the kingdom more than anything else. Jesus is King. He reigns over all. Soon that truth will be evident to all. Until then, kingdom-first living means living like Jesus is King, not you.

How do you "seek first" the kingdom of God?

If you are responding to God with the first five responses—humility, honesty, repentance, forgiveness, and obedience—you *are* seeking His kingdom. Those responses are the language of the kingdom, so just keep learning that language. As you do, the kingdom of God will become more alive to you, more meaningful to you than all the kingdoms of this world. You will come to understand the beautiful but mysterious words of Jesus in this promise: "Do not be afraid, little flock, for your Father has been pleased to give you the kingdom" (Luke 12:32).

He *wants* to give you His kingdom. You are an heir to everything God owns—a joint-heir with Jesus. Stop and thank Him right now. Ask Him to help you start living like everything you own is His so that you can experience life where everything He owns is yours—to use not for your own pleasure, but for His. That is kingdom-first living.

In 2017, Donna and I received a crazy invitation to give up our church, give up our salary, give up almost all we had known, and go on this missionary journey to lead *Life Action*. We were hearing God speak to us, inviting us to go with Him on this journey, but we were afraid—and a little more astonished by all the barriers we would face and the things we would give up than we were by God.

We took a vacation to make our decision. We went to a beautiful beach. One day, I went out for an early morning run, and that morning turned out to be one the strangest, most wonderful, most astonishing times in my life.

A man dropped dead on the beach in front of me. I listened while his son shouted, "Can he be revived?" and watched as paramedics tried to save him. After a while, I ran down the beach for a mile or more and then, overwhelmed by emotion, I sat by a washed-out pier and closed my eyes and wept and sang.

When I opened my eyes, a 75-year-old woman was standing in front of me. I thought she was an angel! But she had simply been resting on the other side of the pier where I couldn't see her. Smiling, she asked me, "Are you singing to the King of kings?'

"Yes!" I said in shock.

"I have a word from Him to you: He's been with you everywhere you have been, and He will be with you where you are about to go."

I wept at this strange miracle as we walked back down the beach together. And I told her my whole story and the decision Donna and I had to make. She told me that she and her husband lived in a condo that shared a wall with the one we were renting for the week. She was a follower of Christ, a daughter of the King. She counseled me as we walked.

When we arrived back where my wife was waiting on the beach, this woman, who might as well have been an angel to me, said, "I'm sure you are ready to make your decision now to lead *Life Action*. After all, today you watched a man die who could not be revived, but there are people and churches everywhere who can be!"

Astonished beyond all imagining, I introduced her to Donna and told her about my morning. Donna and I then went inside, and I called and accepted the presidency of *Life Action*. We had become more astonished by God than we were afraid of anything else!

God speaks. It won't always be as clear to you as it was to us that day on the beach. But He will make sure you understand what He is saying. And then it will be your time, your chance to respond to Him. To the great God. To the great King.

What will you say?

QUESTIONS FOR THOUGHT

1. God is seeking these six key responses from us. Take time to examine your heart.

   • *Humility*
     Are you drawn to self-promotion, self-defense, selfish pleasure, selfish dreams? Read these words: "Humble yourselves before the Lord, and he will lift you up" (James 4:10). What promise does the Lord give to those who choose humility, and what might that promise mean in your life?

   • *Honesty*
     Do you allow others to think you are better than you really are? Do you hide behind a mask of perfection? What are you struggling with most right now? Be real with God about your weaknesses and imperfections. "God chose the foolish things of the world to shame the wise; God chose the weak things of the world to shame the strong" (1 Corinthians 1:27). How can you allow others to know that you do not have it all together?

   • *Repentance*
     Repentance is an active word; it means to turn around and go the other direction. "Repent, then, and turn to God, so that your sins may be wiped out, that times of refreshing

may come from the Lord" (Acts 3:19). What promise does repentance bring to you? Where have you been heading that you need to turn away from? Who or what have you been seeking that you need to turn away from?

- *Forgiveness*
  "If we confess our sins, he is faithful and just and will forgive us our sins and purify us from all unrighteousness" (1 John 1:9). When you choose forgiveness, what does God say He will bless you with? "Bear with each other and forgive one another if any of you has a grievance against someone. Forgive as the Lord forgave you" (Colossians 3:13). How do you respond when others wound you? Is forgiveness a command? If so, what do you hear God saying to you right now?

- *Obedience*
  God speaks. He declares His love. We respond to Him with either a yes or a no. "If you love me, keep my commandments" (John 14:15). This is not complicated, but the battle you face in saying yes is. How astonished are you at God's ways? What is your response to His love?

- *Kingdom-First Living*
  Kingdom-first living means living with Jesus as King, not you. Using that definition, examine your life. "Seek first his kingdom and his righteousness, and all these things will be given to you as well" (Matthew 6:33). Whose kingdom is predominant in your life? What is God's promise to you when you put His kingdom first?

2. When life becomes complicated and giving your yes to God seems difficult, the solution is to develop an overwhelming view of God that captivates your life and heart. You must become

more astonished by God than by anything else in the world. "In the year that King Uzziah died, I saw the Lord, high and exalted, seated on a throne" (Isaiah 6:1). How do you see God right now? Take a moment to see Him as the great and mighty King He is. Can you see Him lovingly waiting for your yes?

chapter three

YES AND NO— BREAKING ADDICTIONS

Donna Avant

Saying yes to God often requires saying no to something or maybe even to someone else.

What is it that you need to put down in order to give a wholehearted YES to what God is asking of you? What or who are you surrounded by that you will need to free yourself from? Is there anything you are giving your devotion to that supersedes your devotion to God?

When our granddaughter Addy yelled, "No!" to her daddy the first time, she was sitting in the middle of her bedroom floor happily playing with her Barbie collection. She was comfortable in her own little messy, pink fortress, surrounded by her dolls and clothes. Playing with her dolls was distracting her from saying yes to her daddy.

The second and third times Addy yelled no to her daddy, she was making a clear choice. She was choosing devotion to her dolls over devotion to her daddy. She had made the decision to allow playing with dolls to control her behavior. From past experiences, Addy knew there would be consequences for saying no to her daddy; but Barbie play was controlling her again.

When a distraction controls our behavior to the point that we are willing to allow negative outcomes, it becomes an addiction. Addy had become a "Barbie addict."

Distractions are plentiful in our world. As I write, my phone is beeping and begging for a response. Yet I am fully aware that if I keep responding to my phone, this chapter and maybe this book will not be completed. Many things distract us from saying yes to what God is asking of us, but those distractions can become addictions if we allow them to control us instead of choosing to control them.

One becomes an addict when they allow a person, a substance, or an emotion to control their lives regardless of any negative consequences that may result.

Addictions come in many different forms. The following is not an exhaustive list, but rather three general categories of addictions.

- **"I" addiction**. An "I" addict is interested in personal comfort and immediate satisfaction. "I do whatever I want, whenever I want." The "I" addict is devoted to self.

  The difficulty in recognizing an "I" addiction is that even good things can be addictive. Addy's Barbie dolls aren't bad or evil; neither are hobbies, exercise, social media, shopping, and even Bible study classes. They can, however, become "I" addiction sources if they pull our devotion, and ultimately our hearts, away from walking in obedience to God.

  If God is asking you to say yes to Him by serving at a local crisis pregnancy center, but instead you enroll in your fifth (or twenty-fifth) Bible study class, then taking Bible study classes may have become an addiction instead of a means to grow closer to the Lord in order to serve Him better. Attending another Bible study may be allowing you to stay in your comfort zone, whereas serving at the local crisis pregnancy center requires you to live out what you have learned in God's Word.

God may be asking you to say yes to Him by increasing your prayer time for others; but if your response is, "I just don't have time," you are making a decision to put other things ahead of saying yes to God. For example, if your day includes ample time to scroll through social media, your devotion to social media may be greater than your devotion to God. Prayer is hard work. Social media brings comfort and enjoyment, easily becoming an "I" addiction.

- **Emotion addiction**. For years I was addicted to the emotion of anger. I had grown up in a home filled with yelling, screaming, and uncontrolled outbursts. If you had asked me when I was sixteen what I wanted most out of life, I would have responded that I wanted a home filled with love, peace, and joy. When I married John, I resolved to establish that kind of home. Yet only a few years into our marriage, my angry outbursts had become a part of our family's daily routine.

Anytime life became too complicated, I responded in anger. Although I couldn't see it at the time, I was addicted to the emotion of anger. I believed that if I yelled loud enough, or threw the right object (without injuring anyone), I could escape the undesired situation in front of me. My anger became a tool of manipulation. If I could scream loud enough, the children would behave. If I threw something across the room, my husband would know I meant what I said.

A clear sign of addiction is becoming defensive when you are confronted by someone who loves you.

Anytime John would attempt to confront me about my anger issues, I would become defensive, declaring, "This is just who I am." I was more devoted to my anger than I was to God, or even to the desire I had for a home filled with peace.

God created emotions, so they are not bad. Scripture tells us that God experiences emotions too (righteous jealousy and anger, to name a few). God's emotions, however, do not lead to addictive or sinful behavior. When our emotions control our behavior negatively, they become addictions.

- **The physical addiction**. When most of us think of addictions, our minds default to bondage. Drugs, alcohol, sex, and food, for example, can become more important to our daily existence than our devotion to Christ. These physical addictions are extremely difficult to break free from because they involve chemical dependency. If you know that you can't go one day without alcohol, cocaine, marijuana, opioids, pornography, or overeating, please know that freedom is available. Recognize your addiction, acknowledge it to someone else, and seek qualified help.

SAY YES TO A RELATIONSHIP WITH GOD

Regardless of the addictions you may struggle with, the first step to freedom is saying yes to a personal relationship with Jesus Christ. My friend Rachel made that choice.

Rachel was born and raised in East Tennessee. Her earliest memories involved her parents' alcohol and drug usage. She did not know what life was like without substance abuse. At age fourteen, Rachel began her own journey with drugs and alcohol. By seventeen she left home to marry her boyfriend, who was also an addict. By twenty she was pregnant by another man and divorced from her first husband. She married her son's father the day before the baby was born, but that marriage ended when her husband began to physically abuse her. Not long after her second divorce, she married a drug dealer and eventually lost custody of her son. In her own words, her life was spiraling out of control.

After divorcing the drug dealer, Rachel met her current husband, Troy, who was also an addict. Rachel told me, "Fun for us was drinking and doing drugs together. We married not long after we met, and I had a baby girl. But with no change in our behavior, our marriage was just a ticking time bomb." The bomb exploded, and a year after their daughter's birth, they divorced. But for the sake of their little girl, they remained friends.

During a trip to the beach, Rachel and Troy discussed what they hoped for and what they would be willing to do in order to change their lives for the sake of their daughter. Troy began watching on television a pastor preaching in Knoxville. He and Rachel decided to attend that church, even though it was an hour away. On September 21 while attending church, Rachel said yes to Jesus Christ and entered into a personal relationship with Him. She then asked Him to break her addictions.

In a recent conversation with Rachel, I asked if she continued to struggle with alcohol and drug abuse after she began her relationship with Christ. She told me, "At first Troy and I just scaled back; but honestly, as we grew in our relationship with Christ, He just removed those desires from our lives." Rachel chose to say yes to a relationship with Jesus, and He broke her addictions!

Not every person who has a physical addiction is released as quickly as Rachel was; however, there is no question that the beginning of freedom from any addiction is choosing to say yes to a relationship with Christ and then no to the addiction.

Rachel chose to run to Jesus as her stronghold instead of to drugs and alcohol.

CHOOSE CHRIST AS YOUR STRONGHOLD

My mentor, Esther Walker, taught me that a stronghold is "anything in our life in which our enemy (Satan) can count on our reaction. The enemy knows how to push our buttons." In 2 Corinthians 10:4, the apostle Paul uses the word *strongholds* to describe addictions.

A stronghold is a place, person, response, emotion, behavior, or substance we turn to instead of turning to God. However, God desires to be your stronghold. Your refuge. Your fortress. Your defense. He does not want anything to control you other than Him. He does not want you to run to anything or anyone else for comfort.

David sang in Psalm 27:1, "The LORD is the stronghold of my life—of whom shall I be afraid?" David wrote this psalm while he was fleeing from King Saul, who was attempting to kill him. During this time, David hid in strongholds—safe places in caves or rocks. David knew that even though he may be hiding in a physical stronghold, God was his true stronghold.

Do you believe you are safer being controlled by your own desires, emotions, or substances? You are not! Decide now to make God your refuge, your fortress. Choose to run into His shelter and away from whatever is gripping your life.

"Abide in me, and I in you," Jesus invites us (John 15:4 ESV). The Greek word *abide* means to "remain under." If you want a stronghold to be broken in your life, run to Jesus, hide in Him, and come under His protection. Choose to make Him your refuge, your *abiding place*!

Are you desperate to be free from the strongholds that are controlling your life? You must come to the end of yourself in order to be freed from your addictions. You must acknowledge your own inadequacy in breaking the strongholds that bind you. John 15:5 says, "If you remain in me and I in you, you will bear much fruit; apart from me you can do nothing." Whatever you can accomplish in this life amounts to *absolutely nothing* without Jesus.

Realizing our inadequacy leads to desperation, and desperation makes us open to change.

FROM DESPERATION TO FREEDOM

Rahab was a desperate woman. Joshua 2 introduces her to us: a prostitute, a woman with some seriously misplaced devotion. But God did not create her or any other woman to live in such bondage.

Rahab's home was built into the city wall of Jericho. I can see her sitting on a window seat, daydreaming about what life would be like beyond the city walls, free from sexual exploitation. I can imagine her thinking, "There has got to be more to life than this. More to life than selling my body every day."

One day, two Israelite spies appeared at her door. Hebrews 11:31 (NKJV) tells us she "received the spies with peace." Rahab was desperate enough to commit treason, by allowing the spies to come inside and by lying to the king's soldiers about their whereabouts, in exchange for freedom from her life circumstances.

I was a desperate woman once. I became desperate for freedom from my emotional addiction the night John came home and said, "Donna, I love you. No matter how much you yell, scream, and throw things, I will never, ever leave you. I am not your dad." (My dad had walked out on my mom when I was sixteen.) Then he added, "Do I want to come home? Not most days. Our home is filled with anger. I want a home of peace."

In that moment I realized that the one thing I had wanted most out of life—a home different than my childhood, a home filled with love and peace—was being sabotaged by my emotional addiction to anger. I became desperate for change.

Desperation will drive you to realize you need a power other than your own to be freed from addiction. Desperation opens your heart and mind to hearing truth. If you are at the point of desperation, I have some very good news. Jesus says to those who believe in Him, "If you hold to my teaching [abide in my word], you are really my disciples. Then you will know the truth, and the truth will set you free" (John 8:31-32).

Our freedom is dependent on our choosing to run to Jesus and His Word as our abiding place, our stronghold. Abiding in His Word means living in it, choosing to be His disciple, following Him, and recognizing our new identity in Him.

A NEW IDENTITY

In Joshua 2, Rahab revealed to the spies that she had heard stories of how God dried up the Red Sea when the Israelites came out of Egypt. She had heard how the Israelites conquered the two kings of Sihon and Og. Rahab told the spies, "Our hearts melted in fear and everyone's courage failed because of you" (v. 11).

After hearing about the God of the Israelites, Rahab began to believe there was Someone stronger than the prostitution that held a grip over her life. She made a decision to believe the truth about God, which caused her to become amazed at God and believe He could be her dwelling place, her stronghold, instead of prostitution.

When Rahab became amazed at who God was, she then began to understand who she really was. She said, "The LORD your God is God [*Elohim*] in heaven above and on the earth below" (v. 11). She declared that the God of the Israelites, the Hebrew God, was truly God. She used the name *Elohim* to identify Him as her Creator. And in accepting *Elohim* as her Creator, she discovered her true identity. She knew that she had been made *by* God and *for* God. She was no longer a prostitute.

Recognizing your true identity is life-changing!

When you take refuge in anything other than Jesus Christ, you are bound to whatever you are identifying with. Rahab no longer identified herself as a prostitute. Instead, she declared, *Elohim is my Creator. I am His.*

In my desperation to be freed from my emotional addiction of anger, I listened as my mentor challenged me not to read God's Word only for knowledge. "Abide in God's Word. Run to it for shelter, for life itself. Make God's Word your stronghold."

I began to consume His Word not for quantity but for quality. As I began to know Him more, I became increasingly amazed at who He is and at His power. I also began discovering my true identity. Although I had come to know Christ as a young girl, I had never really discovered who I am in Christ. I am not just a girl with anger issues from a broken, dysfunctional home. I, Donna Avant, am a daughter of the One True King.

Do you want freedom from your addiction? Decide right now to learn and understand your identity in Christ. Put your name in Romans 8:15-17 and speak it out loud. Declare to the world your true identity:

> I, _____, have not been made a slave, so that I live in fear again; rather, the Spirit I received brought about my adoption to sonship. And by Him I cry, "*Abba*! Father!" The Spirit Himself testifies with my spirit that I am God's child. Now if I am His child, then I am His heir—an heir of God and a co-heir with Christ.[9]

Understanding and believing who I am as a daughter of the one true King gave me the confidence, not in my own ability but in

Christ's ability, to be free from my anger addiction. I was no longer alone in this fight. I did not have to try harder or be better. I had discovered that I have access to the King's power.

THE ROYAL SUPPLY BAG

Several days after Addy had said no to her daddy for the third time and he had corrected her, her daddy observed her once again playing in her room. This time she was walking around with a pretend crown on her head and toting a pink duffel bag. Her daddy asked, "Addy, why are you carrying that bag, and what's inside it?" Addy replied, "It's my royal supply bag. I am a princess, and this bag has all my stuff in it. I'm going to be queen one day."

I love that girl's confidence. Knowing who we are in Christ empowers us with the same confidence. We no longer believe in our own ability; we believe in His. We have our own royal supply bag. It is filled with His power to overcome any addiction in our lives. In 2 Corinthians 10:4, Paul says, "The weapons we fight with are not the weapons of the world. On the contrary, they have divine power to demolish strongholds."

Notice that in his letter to the Romans, Paul first reminds us who we are in Christ—God's children (Romans 8:16). Then he says we are "more than conquerors" (v. 37)! Whatever stronghold is in your life, whatever addiction you may struggle with, God has already conquered it. His victory empowers you to overcome.

> In all these things we are more than conquerors through him who loved us. For I am convinced that neither death nor life, neither angels nor demons, neither the present nor the future, nor any powers, neither height nor depth, nor anything else in all

creation, will be able to separate us from the love of God that is in Christ Jesus our Lord (Romans 8:37-39).

His power is ours. His victory is ours. Our identity in Him enables us to say to no to what enslaves us and to walk in obedience to Him. And being freed from addictions allows us to be a part of His plan.

THE ETERNAL EFFECT OF YES

When the Israelite spies arrived and Rahab recognized that God had sent them, she saw the way to freedom from her bondage. She chose to say no to a life of prostitution. More importantly, she said yes to what God was asking her to do. The Israelite spies needed her help to escape, and she was willing to give it. How awesome is it that someone in bondage enabled the spies to escape!

Amazingly, when people are freed from their strongholds, others around them are empowered to walk in obedience also. The power on display in the lives of those freed from addictions and strongholds empowers others to say yes to God. When the walls of Jericho fell, "Joshua spared Rahab the prostitute, with her family and all who belonged to her, because she hid the men Joshua had sent as spies to Jericho" (Joshua 6:25). Ultimately, Rahab's obedience led not only to her rescue but also to her family's freedom.

The larger story in Joshua 2-6 is the story of what God wanted to accomplish through His people. Jericho had to be conquered so God could fulfill His promise to the Israelites (Joshua 1:6). God also knew that the ultimate purpose of Rahab's life was to be an ancestor of Jesus Christ (Matthew 1:1-5, 16). Rahab did not see the long-term results of her obedience in the centuries ahead, but we now know the eternal effects of her yes to God.

Our yes to God always has a ripple effect on those around us.

A COMPLETE RENOVATION

My deliverance from anger addiction wasn't as dramatic as Rahab's from her bondage, yet it was life-changing for me and my family. After I began to make God's Word my fortress and not just something to read and then check off my Christian to-do list, God began to *renovate* my mind.

From time to time, I watch the TV show *Fixer Upper*. I love to see Chip and Joanna Gaines renovate outdated houses. They tear out the old and replace it with new and beautiful.

Romans 12:2 says, "Do not conform to the pattern of this world, but be transformed by the renewing of your mind." The word *renew* in the Greek means "renovation." But how in the world, I wondered, was this angry, screaming, throwing-things girl going to be transformed? I needed a new mind. I had become desperate enough to desire God's transformation.

First, I had to confess to myself and to God that I had conformed to a pattern of the world by using anger as a tool of manipulation. As I began to abide in God's Word as my fortress, James 1:20 came alive to me: "Human anger does not produce the righteousness that God desires."

My anger was not going to change anyone for the better. My anger was not going to improve my children's behavior. My anger was not going to make John the husband I thought he needed to be. My anger was not going to fix my dysfunctional family. My anger was not going to produce the family life I wanted. My anger was just hurting those around me and would eventually drive them away.

I memorized James 1:20 and wrote it on notecards and placed them around my home. I realized that I literally had to remove the thought patterns I had grown up with and replace them with new patterns of thought. These frequent reminders became part of the process.

The changes didn't appear instantly, but I knew the renovation was in full swing when one day John walked in the door from a long day of work, snuck up behind me as I was cooking, and said, "Donna, I do not know what is going on with you, but you are not the same woman. I wanted to come home tonight."

I still become emotional remembering the joy I experienced when I recognized that God was in the process of freeing me from my emotional addiction to anger. God's powerful Word became the tool that renovated and transformed my mind!

ARE YOU READY TO SAY NO TO YOUR BONDAGE?

If you are struggling with any kind of addiction—if you need to say no to something or someone in order to say yes to God—please know that the power of God and His ability to transform lives is unending.

Rahab was a prostitute. God freed her, and she became an ancestor of Jesus. Rachel was an alcoholic and a drug addict. God freed her. She is now walking with Christ and sharing her story with others. Only God knows how her life will impact generations to come. I was addicted to a lifestyle of anger, and now I am writing a book to help others find freedom in Christ like I am experiencing.

Are you desperate? Are you ready to be freed from your addiction, from whatever stronghold you run to? Are you ready to accept your identity in Christ?

If you are a child of the one true King, say so. Declare your identity to the world around you. Make use of the royal supply bag of power He has provided for you. Choose to abide in His Word. Allow it to renovate your mind so that His power may be displayed in your life. Choose to say yes to God, and say no to whatever grips your life!

If you are not a child of the King, then today is the day for you to surrender to the One who has the ability to set you free.

QUESTIONS FOR THOUGHT

1. What is the difference between a *distraction* and an *addiction*? Is there anything or anyone in your life that is currently a distraction that could become an addiction?

2. Can you identify with having an "I" addiction, an emotion addiction, or a physical addiction? Remember, people become addicted when they allow a person, a substance, or an emotion to control their lives, regardless of any negative consequences that may result. If you have an addiction of any kind, name it specifically. God deals in specifics.

3. The first step toward breaking your addiction is to acknowledge Jesus Christ as your Savior. Have you entered into that relationship? If so, when did you enter into a personal relationship with Him? How closely have you walked with Him since then?

4. Every day, we choose what our stronghold is. We choose to make the Lord our stronghold (our abiding place), or we choose to turn to something or someone else to abide in. Consider these verses:

- "I will say of the LORD, 'He is my refuge and my fortress, my God, in whom I trust'" (Psalm 91:2). Are you trusting in God or yourself?

- "The LORD is the stronghold of my life—of whom shall I be afraid?" (Psalm 27:1). Who or what are you afraid of?

- "Remain in me, as I also remain in you. . . . If you remain in me and I in you, you will bear much fruit; apart from me you can do nothing" (John 15:4-5). What might you have chosen in the past? What is the fruit of your life?

5. How does desperation lead to freedom? Are you at the point where you can say truthfully that you are more desperate for God than for what you are addicted to?

6. Where is your identity? How would you identify yourself? For years I identified myself as a woman with anger issues from a broken, dysfunctional home, who just happened to be a pastor's wife and mom to three children. I found freedom as I learned to identify myself not by my past or my present, but by my relationship to Jesus Christ. Read Romans 8:15 out loud and insert your name into it:

> I, _____, have not been made a slave, so that I live in fear again; rather, the Spirit I received brought about my adoption to sonship. And by Him I cry, "*Abba*! Father!"[9]

7. God identifies you as His child and a *conqueror*. "In all these things we are more than conquerors through him who loved us. For I am convinced that neither death nor life, neither angels nor demons, neither the present nor the future, nor any powers, neither height nor depth, nor anything else in all creation, will be able to separate us from the love of God that is in Christ Jesus our Lord" (Romans 8:37-39). What does this mean to you?

8. Being freed from addictions allows you to be a part of God's plan. Whose plan for your life are you a part of right now? In what area does your mind need renovation? Impurity? Anger? Lust? Gossip? Lack of forgiveness? Identify it specifically. Find a passage of Scripture that speaks truth about that area. Commit that Scripture to memory. Abide in His Word.

chapter four

SAYING YES IN THE MIDST OF SUFFERING

Donna Avant

Elisabeth Elliot defined suffering as "having what you don't want or wanting what you don't have."

Elisabeth Elliot knew suffering. Her first husband, Jim Elliot, was killed by Auca Indians in 1956 as he and four other missionaries (Ed McCully, Roger Youdarian, Nate Saint, and Pete Fleming) were attempting to show the love of Christ to this unreached tribe. The Aucas killed the five missionaries, thinking they came with hostile intent. Elisabeth later married Addison Leitch, who died of cancer four years into their marriage. She then married Lars Gren. Toward the end of her life, she suffered from dementia. She passed away in 2015 at the age of eighty-eight.

This missionary and author clearly was intimately familiar with suffering. She once said, "Suffering is having what you don't want or wanting what you don't have."[10] If anyone else had written this definition of suffering, it might seem simplistic. But Elisabeth knew that suffering comes in many forms relative to the sufferer.

What is in your life right now that you don't want? Or what is it that you want and do not have?

As a sixteen-year-old girl, I remember waking up alone in a two-bedroom apartment, knowing my life was forever changed. My parents had divorced, and our beautiful suburban home was sold. My dad was living in another city with my sister and his new wife. My mom was seeing another man. The family I knew was gone. I had something I didn't want and wanted something I didn't have. *Suffering*.

A precious pastor's wife I know has Chron's disease, rheumatoid arthritis, chronic anemia, and medically induced leukemia. She has something she doesn't want and wants something she doesn't have. *Suffering*.

Friends of mine have a son who has walked away from life in Christ. The young man was raised in a home filled with the love of Jesus, yet he has chosen a lifestyle in direct opposition to how he was raised. This family wants what they do not have. *Suffering*.

A precious young woman I know has just suffered another miscarriage. This one is her third in a few short years. She desperately wants something she does not have. *Suffering*.

These are examples of intense suffering. But there are other examples of suffering that happen in the course of our lives. Some may see them as inconveniences, but nonetheless, while they are occurring, they can be seen as intense to those encountering them.

My middle daughter, Amy, and her husband, Joseph, are currently trying to sell their house. It's been on the market for months. During this time, Joseph has had to drive an hour each way to work. They want something they don't have. That is suffering.

My friends have a daughter, "son-in-love," and their first grandson living in Anchorage, Alaska, where they serve on staff at a church. My friends live in Georgia. Thousands of miles separate them from their only grandchild. They have something they don't want. That is suffering.

As I am writing this, two men are in my kitchen, working on my oven. This trip is their second one to my home in the last two weeks. I have not had a working oven in over a month. I want something I don't have. That is suffering (perhaps mostly for my husband).

Using Elisabeth's definition of suffering, all of us will most likely say we are experiencing some form of suffering. Scripture tells us that at some point, all of God's children will suffer. Romans 8:17 says, "Now if we are children, then we are heirs—heirs of God and co-heirs with Christ, if indeed we share in his sufferings in order that we may also share in his glory."

A good father tends to the wounds of every child, whether it is a boo-boo that needs a Band-Aid or a trauma that requires emergency medical care.

In times when suffering may be more of an inconvenience, God still asks us to say yes to Him. At other times, our suffering may be intense and almost unbearable. In those moments also, He asks us to say yes, even when it seems impossible.

Suffering sometimes makes us want to turn inward. Several years ago, my mom was diagnosed with Alzheimer's disease. Although she and I were not extremely close, she was still my mom, and I loved her. During the last few years of her life, I had to make numerous trips from Tennessee to Texas to help my sister with my mother's care. Many times after coming home from those trips, I would just curl up in a ball on my bed and weep. Watching my mom decline was excruciating.

In times like these, how can we say yes—how can we not only accept our suffering, but also keep trusting God and obeying Him in the midst of it—when all we want to do is retreat into ourselves?

How did Elisabeth Elliot say yes to go back to the Auca Indians to share the good news of Christ with them after they murdered her husband? How did she continue to write books and speak when her second husband was diagnosed with cancer?

How do my friends whose son has walked away from God continue to serve the Lord and love those around them? How does my friend who is a pastor's wife joyfully serve alongside her husband despite her cancer? How was I able to have joy and serve those around me despite living through my mom's Alzheimer's?

The answers lie in understanding the purpose of suffering.

REDEMPTION: A PURPOSE IN SUFFERING

Saying yes to God in the midst of suffering requires us to understand the purpose of suffering. Elisabeth Elliot said, "There is no redemptive work done anywhere without suffering."[11]

The most important redemptive work ever done was when Jesus' blood was shed on the cross, buying us back from sin and death. When we suffer, we are put in the position of becoming like Him in His death—dying to what we want or what we think we want. Whether major or minor, our suffering causes us to realize we can't live without Him. It brings us to the knowledge that we need a Savior.

As I shared in the previous chapter, my childhood home was filled daily with angry explosions. When I was sixteen, my dad left my mom. My mom and dad each married three more times. During the early years of my marriage, Dad would show up on occasion to see his grandchildren. Other times he would commit to coming and then not show up. There were times when he would tell his wife he was coming to see us but then go be with another woman.

When God began a work of revival in 1995 at our church in Brownwood, Texas, that spread across college campuses and into other areas of the United States, John was invited to preach in many churches. During this time, he was asked to speak at a church in the Atlanta area, where my dad was working.

The night before John was to speak, my dad called. "Sugar, I'm in Atlanta. I'm not doing so well. I'm about to be laid off, and

I'm probably going to have to file bankruptcy. Also, my wife [his fourth] is about to leave me."

Dad had reached the end of himself. He was suffering, and he was beginning to realize that he needed a Savior.

I told my dad that John would be preaching the next night at a church in Atlanta. I encouraged him to go hear John and talk to him. Dad agreed to do so. When I told John the news, he did not share my excitement. He knew that my dad had let me down many times by failing to keep his commitments, and he didn't want me to be hurt again.

The next night, when John stood up to speak, he saw my dad sitting toward the back of the church. John had been asked to share about the changed lives in our church, community, and college. At the end of the message, my dad almost ran down the church aisle. He fell into John's arms and said, "John, every good thing God has given me, I have thrown away. Please ask these people to pray for me. I need Jesus in my heart."

My dad entered into a personal relationship with Jesus Christ that night. He had suffered. His suffering led him to the end of himself and straight into the arms of Jesus. Suffering accomplished the work of redemption.

THE FRUIT OF SUFFERING

None of the circumstances in my dad's life changed that night. Yet immediately, his countenance changed. He had hope!

Hope is not a wish or a daydream. **Hope is confident expectation, not that you will get your way, but that God will accomplish His purposes in and through your life.**

The book of Romans contains the word *hope* more than any other New Testament book. At the time of its writing, the church in Rome was experiencing suffering under Emperor Nero. The Roman church needed hope.

Romans 5:3-5 says, "We also glory [rejoice] in our sufferings, because we know that suffering produces perseverance; perseverance, character; and character, hope. And hope does not put us to shame, because God's love has been poured out into our hearts through the Holy Spirit, who has been given to us."

We begin by rejoicing in suffering.

Paul told the Romans that the first step in moving toward hope is to rejoice in who God is. And He closed his letter to the Romans by describing Him as "the only wise God" (Romans 16:27). The Greek word *wise* is the same word the Greeks used to describe a watchman on top of a mountain who had a 360-degree elevated view. God is our watchman! He is not taken by surprise at what is going on in our lives. We can therefore rejoice in our sufferings, not because of the specifics of the suffering, but because of who is watching over us.

Elisabeth Elliot understood this truth when she said, "I never thanked God specifically that certain Indians murdered my husband. I don't think I need to thank God for the cancer or the murder. But I do need to thank God that in the midst of every situation the world was still in his hands."[12]

Do you want to experience hope? Stop right now and begin to rejoice. Declare out loud who God is and His ability to handle any suffering in your life. Acknowledge Him as the watchman in your circumstances.

As we rejoice, suffering begins to produce perseverance in our lives (Romans 5:3-5). I used to think of perseverance as just trying harder or pushing through something. My attitude during times of difficulty was, "I can get through this."

No! God doesn't want us to just "get through" our suffering. He wants us to fully live in Him in the midst of suffering; that's what perseverance is.

To persevere means to "remain under" or "abide." In John 15:5 the same word is used when Jesus says, "If you remain in me and I in you, you will bear much fruit; apart from me you can do nothing." Do you see what God is saying? When we suffer, we will persevere by abiding in Him. When we choose to abide in Him, to remain under Him, He will give us all ability and power not to give up or quit. Our abiding in Him enables us to say yes to Him even when we are suffering.

Scott Hamilton, gold medalist figure skater, shared in an interview: "I calculated once how many times I fell during my skating career . . . 41,600 times. But here's the funny thing: I got up 41,600 times."[13] Scott Hamilton received a gold medal because he did not quit. He chose to get up. Scott chose to persevere in his purpose.

Do not quit! God is looking for men and women who will say yes to Him in the midst of suffering. The Lord wants us to confidently expect that He is working out our lives for His best kingdom purposes. We must choose to believe what Paul said: "We know that in all things God works for the good of those who love him, who have been called according to his purpose" (Romans 8:28).

Several summers ago, I had the privilege of meeting a group of very special women at a retreat overseas. The retreat was being held in a secure location in a country that was not their own. All of the women had lost either a husband, father, brother, uncle, or son to terrorists. Despite their intense suffering, each of these women radiated joy and peace. At times there were tears, but often I saw them smiling and laughing. When I asked through an interpreter, "How can you be filled with joy after you have lost so much?" the answer I heard was, "How can we not, when our Father has done so much for us?"

Every one of these women could have chosen after the conference not to return to their homeland where they had been serving, yet they chose to return to the place where more suffering was likely to occur. When I asked them why they would make that choice, they answered, "How can we not go share with those who do not know? We must return to where so many are hurting and where many are finally coming to know Christ. We do not want our suffering to be wasted."

They rejoiced. They chose to abide in Christ, who holds their ultimate purpose. They persevered.

As a pastor's wife, I can't count how many times the enemy whispered in my ear, "Just quit." My suffering came in the form of negative, complaining, and gossiping people. There were many days I just wanted to run away from them all. But I chose instead to abide in my heavenly Daddy. I would sit in His lap, and He would whisper in my ear, "I know this is hard. But I've got you. You let me love these people through you. Persevere, Donna."

Are you suffering? Do you want to give up on a difficult marriage? A prodigal son or daughter? Your ministry?

Stop for a moment and make the decision that you will not quit whatever God has asked of you. When you persevere, God's Word promises that you will become the real deal.

THE REAL DEAL

According to Romans 5, perseverance leads to character. God is far more interested in our character than our comfort. What does it mean to be a man or woman of character? To put it simply, a man or woman of character is the real deal. Those words describe John and Cindy Cameron.

John and Cindy live in West Monroe, Louisiana. They have been married for thirty-five years. If you ask them how many children they have, their response is, "We have a daughter, Julia, and two sons, Jonathan and Jason. Jason is in heaven."

On a beautiful June day in 2005, Jason and his girlfriend were en route to a volleyball game with friends. A speeding car lost control, crossed the median, and hit their vehicle head-on. Both Jason and his girlfriend were air-lifted to a trauma center. Jason's girlfriend survived, but Jason did not. He was known at home, church, school, and in the community as a leader filled with joy and a passion for Christ.

I asked Cindy how she continues to say yes to God in the midst of intense suffering. She responded:

> In the early days following Jason's death, I found myself in a fog of disbelief. I had so many different emotions. The life I had and always dreamed about had come to an abrupt end. Yet my responsibilities as a wife, mom, and business owner were still present. As a mom, I recognized that Jason lived his life on purpose with the daily mission of sharing the love of Christ with those around him. I made the decision that while I could not understand the circumstances, I would not allow Jason's death to be in vain.
>
> I muddled through each day by totally depending on Christ and the daily disciplines I had developed over the years. I found myself in a continual conversation with Christ, expressing to Him all my fears and questions. Each time, He quieted my broken heart using His Word. In the early days, I learned to simply breathe and take it moment by moment, just "doing the next thing."
>
> During the months to follow, I realized I missed joy. I wondered if I would really ever experience joy again. God reminded me that Jason was joyful because he served others. If I was going to experience joy, I was going to have to begin to serve others again.
>
> God began to give me opportunities to reach out to other parents who experienced the loss of a child. It became my desire that our story would give others hope in the midst of intense suffering.

Cindy chose on a daily basis, sometimes even on a moment-by-moment basis, to abide in Christ, to stay in Him and under Him. She also chose just to "do the next thing," whatever God was asking of her as a wife, mom, and business owner. There were meals to be made, a kitchen to be cleaned, and clothes to be washed. There were business responsibilities and bills to be paid. There was a husband to be loved and two other children who needed her.

The phrase "do the next thing" comes from an anonymous poem Elisabeth Elliot published in *The Shaping of a Christian Family*.

Do The Next Thing

(author unknown)

From an old English parsonage down by the sea,
There came in the twilight a message to me;
Its quaint Saxon legend, deeply engraven,
Hath, as it seems to me, teaching from Heaven.
And on through the hours, the quiet words ring
Like a low inspiration: *Do the next thing.*

Many a questioning, many a fear,
Many a doubt hath its quieting here.
Moment by moment, let down from Heaven,
Time, opportunity, guidance, are given.
Fear not tomorrows, Child of the King,
Trust them with Jesus. *Do the next thing.*

Do it immediately; do it with prayer;
Do it reliantly, casting all care;
Do it with reverence, tracing His hand
Who placed it before thee with earnest command.
Stayed on Omnipotence, safe 'neath His wing,
Leave all resultings. *Do the next thing.*

Looking to Jesus, ever serener
(Working or suffering) be thy demeanor.
In His dear presence, the rest of His calm,
The light of His countenance be thy psalm.
Strong in His faithfulness, praise and sing;
Then, as He beckons thee, *do the next thing.*

What is the next thing God is asking you to do, even though you are in the midst of suffering? Whatever it is, will you say yes?

I am so very thankful for John and Cindy Cameron. Today, Cindy is the leader of GriefShare at their local church. John and Cindy also founded the Jason Paul Cameron Foundation, an organization established in their son's memory. To date the foundation has given hundreds of thousands of dollars in college scholarships and youth camp and mission camp scholarships. Their yes to God in the midst of their suffering continues to produce hope.

A REQUIREMENT FOR HOPE: TRUST

Rejoicing in our suffering brings perseverance, which brings character, which leads us to hope. Hope is something I never really struggled to have until recently.

In the first chapter of this book, John shared about both of us losing our identity: John as pastor and me as a pastor's wife. For me this loss was a form of suffering. I loved being a pastor's wife. I know many might not understand this, thinking I would be thrilled to walk away from the "glass house." Not me. I loved having a position in which I could share the gifts God has given me. I loved having people in my home. I did not want to give that up. I was losing something I had known for thirty-five years, and it was painful. *Suffering.*

During John's last week as senior pastor, my mom passed away due to complications of Alzheimer's. She had fallen and broken her hip, which led to a blood clot. She suffered a major stroke, and after almost a week of being in and out of consciousness, she passed away. *More suffering.*

I was not only losing my identity as a pastor's wife, but I was no longer a daughter to anyone on earth. My heart ached daily. Out of discipline, I rose every morning and ran to my chair, the place where I open God's Word and talk to Him. It was during this time that He led me to the book of Romans to discover that what I needed was hope. I needed to confidently expect that God is still on His watchtower, that God is able to redeem my suffering, and that God is able to use this present suffering for His kingdom purposes.

I read Romans 15:13. "May the God of all hope fill you with all joy and peace as you trust in him, so that you may overflow with hope by the power of the Holy Spirit." I committed it to memory and began to pray this verse over myself and others.

When the Christmas season began that year, the family traditions were especially difficult. Memories of the way it was and the absence of a person I loved haunted me. Every Christmas, I had opened my home to hundreds of people for fellowships . . . but not that year.

John and I kept our tradition of buying and decorating a live Christmas tree not long after Thanksgiving. We put on Christmas music. I made special treats. It was a fun time. As we turned off the house lights to enjoy the beauty of the tree lights, just the two of us sang "Silent Night." My thoughts were, "Yep, this Christmas is going to be silent."

We were in Atlanta for a quick trip to raise support for our new ministry at *Life Action* when I received a text from my husband's assistant, who had been taking care of the house and watering the live tree while we were away. The text was a picture of our seven-foot Christmas tree lying on the floor, with broken ornaments and water everywhere. I just stared at the phone in disbelief as I showed it to John. We were with people, so I held my emotions in check.

When we returned home, we put the tree back up and redecorated it. Fortunately, most of my most precious ornaments were not broken in the fall. After we got the tree up, John retrieved a thirty-five-pound weight from the basement and set it on the base of the tree. No way would that tree fall again.

A week later, after a long day of Christmas shopping, I walked into our home only to find that the tree had once again fallen, and more ornaments were broken.

Suffering. No one died that day. No one had cancer. To some it may have been just an inconvenience. But for me at that moment, it was suffering. I had something I didn't want, and I wanted something I didn't have.

I wish I could tell you that I confidently cleaned up the mess as I quoted Romans 15:13 and was filled with joy and peace. But no. I sat on the floor and sobbed as I yelled at God. In that moment I felt like my entire known world had come apart, and the least God could do for me was keep my tree vertical and my precious ornaments intact.

As I cried, I heard my Abba say to me tenderly, "You aren't trusting Me. I will give you hope, joy, and peace as you trust Me. The promise in Romans 15:13 is conditional. Trust comes before hope, joy, and peace."

As it turned out, the overreaction on my part to the tree incident was just a symptom of my not trusting the Lord for the bigger sufferings in my life at the moment. That's when I began to learn the meaning of the word *trust*.

T.R.U.S.T.

Totally depend on Me. "Donna, you are not 'all in' yet. Abide only in Me. Do not depend on your position, your title, or your salary."

Relinquish all your rights. "Donna, you do not have a right to a Christmas tree, a Christmas party, or even a ministry."

Under My authority. "Donna, come under My authority. Say yes to what I am asking of you."

Sovereignty is Mine. "Donna, I am the watchman on the tower. I see the future, and I know that what I am asking of you is best for My kingdom."

Teachable spirit. "Donna, you need to be teachable. You have become set in your lifestyle and your position. Let Me begin to teach you new and marvelous things. Stand in amazement of Me again."

As I chose to say yes to God in the midst of my suffering, He began to fill me with hope. Not a hope that John would one day pastor again, but the hope of being in the midst of His kingdom work, no matter what it looked like, because I am just His servant.

The Lord also filled me with hope for my mom. I knew she was in heaven. I knew her mind and body were healed. I knew one day I would join her and be able to have a relationship with her like I'd never had on this earth.

Are you trusting God with whatever suffering is in your life? You can trust Him in the small sufferings of life as well as the big suffering. He is a good Father and cares deeply for every wound, no matter how big or small.

HOPE DOES NOT DISAPPOINT

"Now hope does not disappoint, because the love of God has been poured out in our hearts by the Holy Spirit who was given to us" (Romans 5:5 NKJV).

Fellow sufferer, stand under the outpouring of God's love, and be confident that all the pain, the heartache, the disappointment you are experiencing, no matter how big or small, will bring you new hope and increase God's kingdom if you choose to say yes to whatever He is asking of you.

Elisabeth Elliot made that choice.

The Camerons made that choice.

My friends in the Middle East make this choice daily.

Our world is in need of sufferers who are givers of hope to others, using their own pain to advance God's kingdom. God can take your suffering, no matter how messy it is, and allow it to become your greatest message for His glory. So choose to say YES!

QUESTIONS FOR THOUGHT

1. "Suffering is having what you don't want or wanting what you don't have" (Elisabeth Elliot). Using that definition of suffering, write below what you have that you don't want. Then write down what you want that you don't have. Put an asterisk by the ones you consider suffering.

2. "Now if we are children, then we are heirs—heirs of God and co-heirs with Christ, if indeed we share in his sufferings in order that we may also share in his glory" (Romans 8:17). Is suffering optional for a follower of Christ?

3. Hope is expecting with confidence—not that you will get your way, but that God will accomplish His purposes in and through your life. What are you hoping for right now?

4. God is your watchman, according to Romans 16:27. Nothing surprises Him. What is in your life currently that you need Him to handle, to take over? Stop right now and give it to Him. Rejoice in who God is and in His ability to handle any suffering in your life.

5. Is there any circumstance or person you are ready to give up on? What does the word *perseverance* mean to you?

6. When suffering occurs, life still goes on. The Camerons learned how to *do the next thing*. What is the next thing God is asking of you?

7. Review the acrostic T.R.U.S.T. from page 68. Is there one specific area you need to commit to?

chapter five

SAYING YES WITH OTHERS

John Avant

Your yes to Christ must be shared with others. As we reject isolated, self-centered faith, we can experience the type of community Jesus prayed for.

You must say yes to **God** *alone, but you can't say yes to God* **alone**! If that statement sounds like a contradiction, read on.

The word *alone* has multiple meanings, and one is "exclusively." Accepting Christ as your Savior means believing He is the one and only true God. You must believe that He *alone* is God. Assuming you have already done so, you are ready for more.

Alone also means "isolated." The New Testament life of saying yes to God is *not* one lived alone, or isolated from others. Saying yes to God's plan for your life requires a supportive community to encourage and help you.

Donna and I travel frequently for *Life Action*, and we depend on each other for help and support in a variety of circumstances. One day when we were on a flight home, Donna said suddenly, "Oh no! I left my iPad on the last plane! I left it in the seat pocket!"

I was not happy. We couldn't afford to lose such an expensive item. I knew better than to lecture my wife at times like this, but I just couldn't resist. "You need to learn a method to stop losing stuff! When I get on a plane, I count the number of things I am putting in the seat pocket, and I make a silly rhyme like '1-2-3, don't forget me,' and I don't lose stuff. I don't leave our expensive possessions on a plane."

That didn't go so well.

We got off the plane, reported the incident to the airline, and made our way to our car. I could almost see the steam rising from my wife's ears. She said not a word to me all the way to the car. I knew I was in trouble.

Then it got worse.

I got in the car, drove to the gate to pay for our parking, reached in my pocket . . .

I had left my wallet on the plane!

I ran back into the airport, and some nice people were able to retrieve my wallet from the seat pocket before the plane left again. Then I had to make the long walk back to the car to my waiting wife.

I got in, paid for parking, and started the drive home. She held out as long as she could. And then in a very childish, singsong voice, she said, "Well, 1-2-3, don't forget me!"

We decided to laugh instead of fight, but I understood how I had failed her when she needed my support and encouragement.

Some things you can afford to lose in this world, but authentic community—in this case my precious wife—is not one of them. All of us need to live out our faith in the community of others, where we can expect their support and encouragement.

A SUPPORTIVE COMMUNITY

Yet another meaning for *alone* is "lonely." This may indeed be the loneliest time in American history.

A study published by a leading health insurance company shows that American loneliness is at an epidemic level.[14] Almost half of Americans feel lonely and left out. And it's not getting better. In fact, Generation Z, or those born between 1995 and 2015, are the loneliest generation, with Millennials close behind. So the younger you are, the lonelier you tend to be.

Those who call themselves followers of Christ cannot accept this lifestyle passively. We are called to follow our Lord, the friend of sinners, and help the lonely find a place of love and family in this world. But we can't do that if we are living our lives alone. It is easy for believers to become busier and busier and then decide to back away from the church, including small groups and other relational opportunities. But if we abandon community, we abandon the mission of Christ.

Jesus told us what matters most to Him about the church today. In John 17:20, He prayed to His Father specifically for us: "My prayer is not for them [His current disciples] alone. I pray also for those who will believe in me through their message."

What did He ask His Father to do for His disciples? "That all of them may be one, Father, just as you are in me and I am in you. May they also be in us so that the world may believe that you have sent me" (v. 21).

Think about what Jesus was saying here. He could have asked His Father for any number of things when He prayed for His present and future followers. But the one thing He asked for is that we will be together in unity.

This prayer request is not just a sentimental wish from Jesus for everyone to have a friend. Jesus says the purpose is so that those who don't know Him will see how His followers shatter barriers, come together in community, and love each other. As a result, they will want in on whatever it is these believers have in common.

You and I have the opportunity to be a part of that kind of unity. As we reject isolated, self-centered faith, we can experience the type of community Jesus prayed for.

As a ministry, we at *Life Action* dream of seeing "millions of God-astonished lives, in action with Him, shattering divisions, injustice, and lostness." We believe this dream is a contemporary re-defining of revival. It is what the church would look like if revival came to the body of Christ.

Imagine what might happen in our nation. It's difficult to imagine any problems our society faces today that would not be either solved or greatly reduced.

Real New Testament community would shatter the dark barriers of racism and classism. It would address the violence in so many communities, as people became protective friends and neighbors again. It would begin to heal our broken families, as unity would become the top priority. Within our churches, people would be free to serve and bless in the power of the Spirit rather than spend their time fussing and fighting about lesser things.

This is not a hopeless dream. Revival has happened many times in history. The first-century church in Rome is one example. Darkness pervaded the culture. All the evils and moral degradation we see in America today were present, and sometimes more. Abortion, infanticide, slavery, and sexual depravity were accepted as normal. Believers had no power whatsoever to do anything about these evils politically. And the government? We think we have problems now. Imagine life with Nero on the throne!

With all these circumstances, the believers did not complain about how mistreated they were. The government threatened them, imprisoned them, tortured them, took their possessions, enslaved them, and killed them. The only thing the government could not do was stop them from living out their faith in community with others. And against all odds, they transformed an empire!

How did the believers in Rome pull this off? More importantly, how did they keep saying yes to God with so much against them?

The answer is straightforward. They didn't say yes to God

on their own. They kept their hearts, homes, families, and futures shared in community.

Compare this picture of the early church to the "come for an hour twice a month" experience of so many Christians in churches today:

> They devoted themselves to the apostles' teaching and to fellowship, to the breaking of bread and to prayer. . . . All the believers were together and had everything in common. They sold property and possessions to give to anyone who had need. Every day they continued to meet together in the temple courts. They broke bread in their homes and ate together with glad and sincere hearts, praising God (Acts 2:42-47).

Do you see the common thread of the early church's behavior? *Fellowship, together, in common. Sharing, in each other's homes, at the temple together.*

And the results?

They had "the favor of all the people. And the Lord added to their number daily those who were being saved" (v. 47).

The believers had *favor* with people who didn't know Jesus. They weren't their enemies. They were their friends. Day by day they worshiped *together*, so day by day more people were drawn to the Lord with them.

And the results of their actions didn't stop when new believers were added to their numbers. The unity of the church, the contagious community, continued to grow. Acts 4:32 says, "All the believers were one in heart and mind. No one claimed that any of their possessions was their own, but they shared everything they had."

All of the believes rejected isolation and knit their hearts and souls together. They became an unstoppable force! "With great power the apostles continued to testify to the resurrection of the Lord Jesus. And God's grace was so powerfully at work in them all" (v. 33).

If you and I want this result, we have to pursue a supportive community among ourselves, at least as strongly as these early believers did.

In an age when you can lie on your sofa and watch great preaching as long as you want, find any kind of biblical instruction online while alone in your living room, and have 5000 "friends" through social media without actually spending a minute together with them, you will have to actively choose a supportive community.

It will be a counter-cultural decision. It will not be easy. You may have to sacrifice other priorities that could be costly to you. But here's a crucial question: Is it important to you to be part of the answer of Jesus' prayer?

And here's another one: Wouldn't it be worth sacrifices to have the kind of community life the early believers had, like we read about in the book of Acts?

If the answer to these questions is yes, then take action. Move away from isolation and toward community.

HAGGAI'S EXAMPLE

I love the story of community in the book of Haggai. Bible scholars don't know a lot about this man named Haggai. They know he preached his first sermon on August 29 in 520 B.C. They also know that the people listened to his preaching and did what the Lord said. That in itself was pretty rare for Old Testament prophets. But most importantly for us, we know that, as the community of God's people in this short book said yes, they continued the chain of divine events that led to our salvation today.

Here's the story. The people of Judah had lived in Babylonian captivity for a generation. But by God's grace they were being freed to return home to rebuild the temple of God, to become the people of God in Jerusalem again.

Hurrah, right?

But sadly, most of the people had become comfortable in Babylon and chose to stay there. (It can be easier to stay in the slavery of a comfortable culture than to move boldly and obediently in a new direction.)

Even more sadly, those who went back to Jerusalem didn't fully embrace their role as the "people of God." They immediately began to build their own suburban houses and take care of themselves. They were missing the opportunity to be the people of God *together*—for God first, not self.

But God had a word for them through His prophet Haggai: "Is it a time for you yourselves to be living in your paneled houses, while this house remains a ruin?" (Haggai 1:4).

I hear God speaking. Do you? I hear Him calling us to community—to believe that "me without you" just doesn't work. Consider this challenge to a corporate "yes to God" as a doorway into the *real* "good life."

Decide together to reject self-centeredness.

Saying yes to self never satisfies. Look around at the evidence. Every day we see another story of a celebrity with more money than we can dream of who dies young or ends up in jail or the hospital. People who have the most money, the most sex, the most potential for pleasure, end up in rehab centers and counseling. The enemy keeps whispering to us that we can satisfy ourselves on our own. But that's just an invitation to be stupid. If we know God, we know a better way.

Choose a community of faith as the center of your life.

Radically confront and reject anything that threatens unity in Christ as an attack of the enemy, including gossip, sporadic attendance, anonymity, disengagement, viewing church as enter-tainment, and so on. Read Acts 2 and 4 again, and then find a church fellowship like that one, or help yours become a church like that, or help start a church like that.

Make a "holy pause" part of the normal flow of your life.

"This is what the LORD Almighty says: 'Give careful thought to your ways'" (Haggai 1:7). This was the second time the Lord said these words in seven verses. He meant business. The phrase means to stop and meditate on your life.

Most people never really pause to hear God. I learned a long time ago that I have to have regular times—whole days to get alone and listen to God. The New Testament records Jesus intentionally seeking time alone to pray (John 6:15; Matthew 14:13). If Jesus needed it, I do too.

I need these times for my marriage as well. Donna and I take time every January to evaluate our relationship, and make changes to pursue the marriage God wants us to have. How much more I need these times with Christ to evaluate my relationship with Him!

What about the life of the church? A church can get so busy with so many programs that the average participant can't keep up with them all. Fewer people are coming to any of them. Is it time for your church just to stop and hear God, to take a "holy pause"?

How did the people of Judah respond to Haggai's "Thus says the LORD of hosts"? They made a decision. They stopped and considered their ways, and they decided to obey God together. The leaders "and the whole remnant of the people obeyed the voice of the LORD their God" (1:12). What happened next? They came together and began to build the temple again. The people of God said yes to God Himself as the center of their life.

Live intentionally and exclusively for God's YES.

When God's people said yes to Him, He spoke His yes over them: "'I am with you,' declares the LORD" (1:13).

Ask yourself, what else could you possibly need? For God to say yes over your life, to be *with* you through all that you face? Yes! Live for that! Pursue it with others you can trust. And when one of you fails, forgive, and trust each other again. Keep pursuing community as you follow Jesus.

The people of Judah listened to God and said yes. Then God spoke again, telling them that eternal things were happening because of their obedience. "This is what the LORD Almighty says: 'In a little while I will once more shake the heavens and the earth, the sea and the dry land. I will shake all nations'" (2:6-7).

Obviously, the significance of this moment is about more than rebuilding a building. It is about what happened in the centuries that followed. Because God's people chose to become obedient to Him again, one day the Messiah came forth from these people!

They had no idea the effect they would have on history by doing the hard thing—by rejecting selfish isolation and coming together as a community to obey God. Aren't you glad they said yes to God?

Sometimes it will be hard for you too. You may have to sacrifice to say yes to God together. But even if it's painful, remember this: Don't lose heart when things are hard—you might be changing the world.

We now live in a time of both greater knowledge and greater responsibility. We know that the gospel is for everyone, and that we are charged to share it with everyone—and that it saves like nothing else. "Therefore he is able to save completely those who come to God through him, because he always lives to intercede for them" (Hebrews 7:25).

"Save completely." He has done that for me. And for you. Did He also do that for our neighbors? For strangers? Even for our enemies?

It is easy to not care. All we have to do is keep doing what we normally do—live our life and let others live theirs. Except we're really not saying yes to God if we are headed to heaven without making any effort to make sure others are going too.

The very mission Jesus stated for His life on earth was this: "The Son of Man came to seek and to save the lost" (Luke 19:10). How can we claim to say yes to Him and follow Him if we aren't joining Him in going after the lost?

Our yes must be shared. We are not meant to live our life alone or to leave those who are lost alone, without Christ forever.

When you said yes to God for the first time, you did the most important thing in the world and received the greatest gift of all. But you must not keep that gift to yourself.

FEELING ALONE

If you determine to share the love of Jesus with others, to join Him on His mission, at times you may very well feel alone. Not everyone will go with you on your journey.

But you are not alone. The Lord said in Matthew 28:20 that when we make disciples, when we share His love with others, He is with us, always.

I have a Middle Eastern friend who has determined to share the gospel anywhere with anyone, even at risk to his life. A few years ago, he led a radical Muslim to Jesus. As is happening so often these days, this Muslim man had been having dreams of Jesus, which led him to my friend in a supernatural way.

After this once-radical Muslim came to faith, he began to share his testimony with everyone who would listen, and even with those who would not. This man asked my friend to baptize him (I will call him Haseem) and his wife in their house in a metal water tank. Haseem invited all his Muslim neighbors to come watch, even knowing the danger he would be in. At his baptism he called all his neighbors to come to Jesus. His wife proclaimed, "This is a Jesus house now!"

Haseem lived only a short time after this before he was murdered by some of the people who had witnessed his baptism. His wife is being cared for and remains a vibrant witness.

This is so hard to understand! Why would the Lord allow Haseem to say yes to Him *alone* and then to die *alone*?

Not long ago, some missionary friends of mine went back into the region where Haseem was martyred. As far as they knew, there were no believers in that area after Haseem was killed. I had a chance to visit with them in the Middle East where they live. They could not wait to tell me the story of their visit to Haseem's home. I asked, "Did you find any Christ-followers that have come to Jesus because of Haseem's martyrdom?"

"We found twenty-six," they said.

"Twenty-six!" I shouted. "That's a miracle!"

One of the missionaries stopped me. "You interrupted us. We didn't find twenty-six Christians. We found twenty-six *churches*! Each one is pastored by a former Muslim who came to Christ because of the testimony and the death of Haseem!"

Haseem was *not* alone. The King of everything was with him. And his yes is still changing that region today.

Your yes to God may not be as dramatic or as dangerous as Haseem's, but if you are willing to risk, to love enough to not stay silent, to refuse to go to heaven alone if you can help it, then there will be lonely moments. But you, like Haseem, will never be alone. God will be taking your yes and creating from it a miracle. And maybe a multitude.

It is not always an easy thing to say yes to God. But it is a glorious thing. And it is always worth it.

QUESTIONS FOR THOUGHT

1. Jesus prayed, "My prayer is not for them alone. I pray also for those who will believe in me through their message, that all of them may be one, Father, just as you are in me and I am in you. May they also be in us so that the world may believe that you have sent me" (John 17:20-21). Why did Jesus ask the Father for what He did? How are you choosing to be a part of the answer to Jesus' prayer?

2. "They devoted themselves to the apostles' teaching and to fellowship, to the breaking of bread and to prayer. . . . All the believers were together and had everything in common. . . . Every day they continued to meet together in the temple courts . . ." (Acts 2:42-47). Why might you be struggling with loneliness or isolation? What is God's answer to loneliness and isolation?

3. How is the community of faith at the center of your life helping you on your journey? What is keeping you from choosing to do more with other believers?

4. God said in Haggai 1:7, "Give careful thought to your ways." This phrase means to stop and meditate on your life. To what extent do you think your life right now is what God intends it to be? When is the next time you can take a "holy pause" to examine your life, your marriage, your family, your interactions and fellowship with other believers?

5. In the book of Haggai, when God's people said yes to Him, God spoke His yes over them: "'I am with you,' declares the Lord" (1:13). If you are not living your life intentionally and exclusively for God's yes, what is stopping you?

6. "The Son of Man came to seek and to save the lost" (Luke 19:10). Jesus came to earth to go after those who do not know of His love, His peace, His power. Going with Jesus on His mission requires seeking the lost along with Him. Who do you know right now who is lonely and living apart from Christ? Choose today to seek them out and share the love of Christ.

chapter six

THE MISSION OF YES

Dan Jarvis

[We asked our friend Dan Jarvis to write this chapter, to illustrate what your life can become if you accept the invitation of this book. Dan serves with us at Life Action *and helps our message team develop and deliver life-changing content.]*

I've spent the last few years studying what it means to say yes to God in every category of life. It's one thing for my yes to God to fit nicely into church, or within my ministry contexts, or around the dinner table at prayer time. But what about when yes requires sacrifice? Or when it calls me outside of my normal routine, or away from my self-made priorities and into a kingdom-first mindset?

As a pastor, I'm charged with leading people to follow Jesus, of course; and as a *Life Action* staff member, I talk with other pastors all across the world about what biblical obedience looks like, and how to create contexts that help people move in that direction. I've started to realize that Christian obedience is a school from which I'll never graduate. There's always another lesson to learn, another level to unlock.

Each time I say yes to God, I take another step forward. You can too.

INTO THE COMFORT ZONE

My parents turned to Christ in dramatic fashion when I was a pre-teen. Mom shifted from secular to sold out, and shortly thereafter, Dad turned to Christ out of a life of drugs and difficulty. From then on, we were all in. Dad worked at a printing company and, in the first few weeks of his new faith, had a bumper sticker created that said, "MIRACLES HAPPEN: Ask Jesus for details."

Dad's bumper sticker came to life in some amazing ways. Throughout my teen years, I saw a faith-based *yes* in my parents as they did things that were crazy by the world's standards (and by some church standards too). Mission trips to Asia, ministering to the down-and-out, inviting homeless Russians to live in our house, knocking on neighborhood doors to give out Gospel of John booklets, attending anything and everything the church offered, strategizing to get children's gospel literature into foreign countries . . . It was a whirlwind and tons of fun. Miracles *did* happen!

Sometimes when I tell the stories from that era, they seem almost unbelievable . . . so much so that occasionally I have to remind myself, *Wait, those things actually happened. I was there!*

One memory I hold dear is of my mother, struggling to say yes to a call God had put on her heart to start a ministry. She believed the Lord had given her a name for it: Comfort Zone. But in this particular instance, she was saying no to God because it seemed too much for her new faith. You see, as a younger woman, she'd had an abortion; and although her secular worldview had allowed for it, her conscience hadn't.

For her, those years in the early 1980s were defined by many sleepless and sad nights, wondering what could have been, unable to forgive herself, sinking deep into depression, and living in constant fear that God—whom she believed in conceptually but not in a personal way—would somehow strike back at her.

Upon becoming a Christian, however, my mom experienced the incredible forgiveness of Jesus and started to feel freedom and joy again. She was released from guilt by the mercy of God. She knew there were millions of other women in her generation who had bought into the lie of "convenience abortion," and she suspected that they also struggled deeply in secrecy and fear.

That's when she heard God say, "Why not start a ministry to help these women find freedom?"

Then, her fear crept back in. *If I start this ministry, I'll have to tell my friends at church that I had an abortion. What will they think of me? Will they even accept me, knowing what I did to my baby?*

The battle raged for weeks in her heart.

Finally at a breaking point, she needed to hear God's voice definitively. On a particular Sunday night at our church, while a missionary from the area called Yugoslavia at that time was speaking about the condition of his work, my mom whispered a fleece-type prayer[15] to the Lord: "If he uses the phrase *comfort zone*, I'll know You want me to start this ministry."

She was sure the missionary wouldn't say it on his own. After all, Yugoslav missions were about as far away from her life as one could possibly get. But can you guess what happened? "To minister in my country, you have to step outside of your *comfort zone . . .*"

My mom burst into tears, finally surrendering to the Lord, knowing it meant revealing her secret to the world.

The Comfort Zone ministry she started went on to help a number of women struggling with post-abortion guilt, and it ultimately led to my mother becoming the women's chaplain of our county jail, a post she still holds today in Medina, Ohio. Her risky *yes* has since resulted in thousands of women hearing about Jesus and the hope He offers, and it reverberates today in countless lives.

You never know where your yes will lead, and what God will do when, fully and finally, you surrender to Him.

AN ADVENTURE TO LIVE

A *yes to God* life will lead you to places you never expected to go, with people you would never have otherwise met. Like the heroes of faith in Hebrews 11, your *yes life* is an adventure from start to finish, with plot twists galore. That's why yes requires faith, because there's no way to anticipate what's around the corner. The writer of Hebrews recounts adventures average men and women experienced by saying yes:

> Through faith [they] conquered kingdoms, admin-
> istered justice, and gained what was promised; who
> shut the mouths of lions, quenched the fury of the
> flames, and escaped the edge of the sword; whose
> weakness was turned to strength; and who became
> powerful in battle and routed foreign armies.
> Women received back their dead, raised to life again.
> There were others who were tortured. . . . They were
> put to death by stoning; they were sawed in two;
> they were killed by the sword. . . . They wandered
> in deserts and mountains, living in caves and holes
> in the ground. These were all commended for their
> faith (Hebrews 11:33-39).

Many of these adventures came at high personal costs. Consider Paul's adventure and the many perils he experienced following Jesus. He was one of the most fruitful gospel ministers in his generation and among the greatest people of faith in history. But he also paid a high price for his yes:

> Three times I was shipwrecked, I spent a night and
> a day in the open sea, I have been constantly on the
> move. I have been in danger from rivers, in danger

from bandits . . . in danger in the city, in danger in the country, in danger at sea (2 Corinthians 11:23-28).

As history informs us, Paul's *yes life* ended in martyrdom, as did many of those first- and second-century Christians who gave their all to see God's kingdom expanded. But a love-filled, kingdom-first, high-impact, slightly shorter *yes life* is far more of an adventure worth living than a boring, selfish, predictable, and slightly longer *no life*.

Jesus said people who cling to their lives end up losing what matters most (Matthew 10:39). Those who give up their lives for the sake of Christ end up gaining more than they ever could have expected.

Adventure awaits for any who agree to the simple terms of faith. You can be a scholar like Paul or a fisherman like Peter—no matter. God will take your humble yes and multiply its meaning far beyond what you would ever know to ask for or what your mind could ever imagine.

YES, ONE MORE TIME

My wife and I met at *Life Action* in the early 2000s. One of our shared goals early on was to use our family as a context for ministry. From an early age, Melissa had been a fan of George Müller, the famous Englishman who started an orphanage in prayerful faith. By age nine, she was dreaming of a day when she could do the same thing.

Soon, we were sitting in foster-parenting classes, thinking about what kind of children we could say yes to and what kinds of needs we could meet. Before long, we held a beautiful newborn boy in our arms, and we were in for a crash course on parenthood. For a few weeks, we loved him dearly and treated him as our very own, but in our hearts we knew he couldn't stay. His biological mother was working things out, and it was important that she receive him back as soon as possible so that his young bonding could happen with her rather than with us.

I'll never forget the moment I handed him to her for the last time. I was crying, yet hopeful that his future would be bright. It still hurts to remember that moment.

That day marked a difficult decision for us, and it illustrated to us both the joy and the cost of saying yes to God's call. If we were going to be foster parents, it wasn't going to be romantic and wonderful; it was going to be gritty and challenging—perhaps unfulfilling in the worst way possible.

We almost gave up.

Then the phone rang again; another newborn needed us. With trepidation and guarded hearts, we took a deep breath and said yes.

I'm so glad we did. Today that newborn is our thirteen-year-old son, Noah—who has spent every day of his life, except that very first one, as part of our family. I sometimes wonder if I had been in a bad mood that day, or particularly busy, or if my wife and I weren't getting along in that moment, what might have happened. What if we had said no?

I don't necessarily think that the answer to every offer and every opportunity should be yes for a Christian, but I've resolved in my own heart to "lean yes" whenever I feasibly can. And I'm blessed with a wife who thinks the same way.

Forty foster children later, six of whom we've adopted into our family, I can say that the road has been exactly what we might have predicted at the beginning: devastatingly painful, and incredibly joyful. Sometimes "the best of times and the worst of times" literally are happening at the same time in the Jarvis house.

We've run the gambit: from a teen girl who was a "cutter" that we had to drive to a psych hospital for intervention, to a second-grader who prayed in our guest room to receive Jesus. We've nursed wounds, picked up puking kids at school, attended counseling appointments, shared laughs around the dinner table with children who never had a father figure before, shown our wedding video to wide-eyed kids who just thought I was "the boyfriend" and had no idea what getting married was, broken up fights, and held crying children who didn't know what was going to happen next.

We've dealt with fetal alcohol syndrome and reactive attachment disorder—which, when mixed together, is about as bad as anything I can imagine for a young life and for anyone around them. We took in a girl late one Christmas Eve and had to scramble to wrap some extra presents so she could have some semblance of a merry Christmas morning. Another little boy was found crying in an apartment alone, in nothing but a dirty diaper. An officer brought him to the station, and we got a call about a six-month-old who needed our help. I arrived to find a one-year-old waiting for me, sitting next to an officer who wasn't very good at guessing ages.

We've been registered at the hospital as grandparents to the baby of a foster daughter, even though we were only eleven years older than she was. (Prior to that birth, the girl had been taken to an abortion clinic by her boyfriend, under pressure to end the child's life. She called Melissa from the waiting room just before going in for the procedure, pleading for help. Thankfully, at the last minute, our "daughter" chose life.)

Being attached to the foster parenting community landed me in court as a witness to "how bad it was when they came into our care"; brought us up close and personal with some of the best and worst of humanity; showed us the horrifying impact of drugs and alcohol; and connected us to children, families, and social workers we would never have otherwise met.

One *yes* has led to another, and to another. Since then, we've seen many of our family and friends jump into the foster and adoptive care community, pledging to "love one more" as God provides, extending the echoes of *yes* far beyond what we'll ever realize.

As of this writing, we have ten children in our home—and a few others around the edges who aren't exactly in our family but who hang with us quite a bit. It's not quite George Müller, but my wife's childhood vision is slowly coming to pass.

People frequently ask us if we're "done" yet with all of this. On a practical level, I know what they're asking, and I'm not actually sure. We're trying to say yes to God, not to our own impulses or to the expectations of others. He might want us to love one more within our family, or He might have in mind other ways for us to keep loving others, as life changes seasons and as the complexities of our tribe grow (they are becoming teens).

WELL DONE

Technically, I don't feel freedom to say, "We're done," until Jesus says, "Well done." Having surrendered to Jesus, my destiny is in His hands, not my own. Declaring "I'm done" sounds suspiciously like *no*, which is why I'm trying to approach new challenges with humility. If the past has taught me anything, it's that I have no idea what the future holds.

I don't think every challenge that presents itself should be answered with yes, nor do I think every Christian should offer the same yes as we have—or as John and Donna have, for that matter. Each of us is called to our own mission within the Great Commission. For you, it could be global outreach, advancing in your career field to be a light for the gospel, finishing your education to be equipped for next steps, mentoring young people, starting a church, befriending your neighbors, or a host of other things.

But as for the Great Commission itself, your answer and mine must always be *yes*. We then have the joy of seeing how it will play out in our lives, as empowered by the Holy Spirit.

I was once in a training session for strategic ministry planners (people who help churches and non-profits determine their goals), and they had us walk through an exercise of imagination. The idea of the exercise is to help people think through the process it will require to see their vision become reality. At first I thought it was a little cheesy, but it has grown on me. Try it:

Imagine where you want to be, and then imagine a future time when you actually arrive. You succeed at what you're dreaming of. Someone asks you, "So, how did you do it? How did you succeed?" What are some of the things you can imagine saying in that moment?

Jesus paints a picture for us of a future moment when He will say, "Well done, good and faithful servant!" (Matthew 25:21).

This exercise got me thinking: *What if I applied that same vision exercise to my Christian life?* So I decided to walk through the exercise with that as my end-point vision. Here is what came to my mind.

Jesus has just said to me, "Well done, Dan, my good and faithful servant. Enter into My joy!" I can hardly contain my excitement as I give my Lord a big hug, or a humble bow. I step over a threshold, and a gate is opened into the wondrous, colorful, everlasting joy of the Lord.

Someone walks up and says, "Dan, so great you are here! Thank God for His grace, right? But say, I'm curious. Jesus commended you for being a faithful servant. What exactly did you do, to be faithful to Him?"

Hmmm.

What did I do, during my earthly life, to be faithful to my Lord?

What did I think about? What motivated me? What did I prioritize?

How did I answer the people who told me to quit? What did I do when hard times came along? What was my answer to God's call then?

Jesus' "Well done" is not dependent on you being creative or pithy or original. It's about being *obedient*. It's about daily faithfulness. It's about saying yes when the crowd is counseling you to say no, and pressing forward when every bone in your body wants to shrink back. It's about having faith that Jesus will meet the needs that arise during your *yes life*.

Jesus might call you into the ordinary, or He might call you to something complicated. He might ask you to be faithful in what you think are "little things," serving in the kitchen at church, making dinner for a neighbor. He might call you to something that involves suffering of some kind, or He might call you to stand on a platform and proclaim truth to millions.

In any event, God calls you to say yes to Him. As the old song says, "When Your Spirit speaks to me, with my whole heart I'll agree, and my answer will be yes, Lord, yes."[16]

A MOUNTAINTOP EXPERIENCE

It's not often that guys like me end up in the remote villages of India, and the story of how I got there involves a whole chain of yes moments.

My mission team landed near Nasik, India, and hopped on a bus for a two-hour ride into the arid hills of Maharashtra. Passing by oxen and motorcycles, Hindu temples and country thatch huts, we wound our way up and down roads in varying stages of development until we parked in a field, where the road ended.

"We walk from here," our guide announced.

Our team hiked up a dusty foot trail to a village that was just getting electricity for the first time. Half-naked children ran in the common area, some stopping in curiosity to gawk at us, others chanting things in their local dialect, expecting that we'd understand. I was there to help dedicate a new church building, which was the first of its kind in the area. Just a few years prior, the gospel came to this village community for the first time, and about 25% of the area turned to Jesus.

I didn't deserve to be there, by my account, and I certainly didn't deserve the opportunity I was given to speak a few words of blessing, through a translator, to the gathered villagers about their new church location. But "Yes, Lord" took me there, and it was a moment I'll never forget.

Someone from my team took a picture that I reflected on later, wondering, *How did I, Dan Jarvis, end up in this picture?* After all, this particular village is about as far away from my earthly home as I could possibly wander—literally on the other side of the world.

And yet, it happened. How?

Well, as a pre-teen, I said yes to Jesus and to His ownership of my life. That was the kickoff. Then I said yes to getting involved with Great Commission activity globally, and yes to some church opportunities in that vein over the years. Then there was the invitation to this particular trip, during which I was to help train village pastors who lacked seminary education.

All of those yes moments converged into this one snapshot of an unforgettable adventure to a mountaintop on the other side of the world.

As I peruse my photo history, I can find other pictures like that one—pictures of people I've loved, places I've gone, experiences I've had, and lessons I've learned. I wouldn't have even known I wanted to do any of this before it happened.

MISSING THE MOUNTAINTOP

If someone had asked me in advance, I might have been tempted to say, "No, thanks," to some of the crazier stuff I've experienced on mission with Christ. Or, "That will never work." Or, "That wouldn't really happen." Or, "I'm not ready for that." Or, "I'd never be able to afford it."

Maybe that's why God doesn't give us the whole story ahead of time, and why He lets us learn as we go. He just invites us to say yes, and then our photo albums get a lot more interesting.

I can point to many photos of amazing things that happened when I said yes to God. You probably could do the same, if you and I were looking through your albums. I'm sure there would be a lot to share if we got together and compared all of the unique stories.

But wait, I ask myself. *What about that time I said no to God?*

What about the photo that could have been taken, of the place I could have been, of the person I could have loved? What about the opportunity I missed because in that moment I was thinking of myself, of my own plan, rather than yielding to God? Or I was wasting time in some frivolous sin?

Was there an adventure to live, that I left on the table? Was there a person God wanted me to serve, or an assignment He wanted me to enthusiastically embrace? Was there something I was supposed to learn?

Truth be told, I've said no more than once, and not in the healthy sense of saying no for the sake of priorities or work/life balance. I've said no when I knew God wanted a yes. And that's the no that concerns me.

Have you ever tried to load a photo that just won't show up, maybe because it wasn't linked correctly or because your Internet service was down? In that moment, what do you see? It usually presents as a gray or white box. The placeholder is there, but no picture. Something colorful and alive and meaningful was meant for that space, but instead, nothing.

I don't want my life's album to be full of blanks like that. It's not that I live in constant regret; it's just worth thinking about. We tend to emphasize the costs associated with saying yes to God, but there's an even higher cost we pay when our stubborn hearts say no or "not yet." Or, "I'll do it my way."

Someday, when we are casting our crowns before Jesus, imagine that we also could have an opportunity to hand Him our life in pictures—the snapshots of the things we hold most dear, all of the amazing opportunities He gave to us.

YES TO YOUR MISSION

I've been a writer for my entire Christian life, all the way back to my early teen years. I was so excited about the mission opportunities I was hearing about in my church that I started a little newsletter called "Your Mission" to distribute to the members. I would sit at our family's Apple II computer and, in between feeding the dog and annoying my sister and begrudgingly doing chores around the house, I'd peck out little articles about anything and everything related to the Great Commission.

It was simplistic, but when I look back at it, I wonder if I haven't complicated things for myself in the years since. The mission is simple, right? Just yes, every day.

Honestly, it excites me to be in a constant state of discovery. It's fun to ask God, "What's on the docket for today, Lord? What's my next step?" Aren't you curious about that too? The God of the universe loves you deeply and went to great lengths to save you, and He has good works prepared for you to do. What are they?

Mountaintops in India?

Foster children at the police station?

Something more than you'd ever ask or think to ask? Who knows!

I love how Paul described his mission, and by extension, yours and mine:

> If it seems we are crazy, it is to bring glory to God. And if we are in our right minds, it is for your benefit. Either way, Christ's love controls us. Since we believe that Christ died for all, we also believe that we have all died to our old life. He died for everyone so that those who receive his new life will no longer live for themselves. Instead, they will live for Christ, who died and was raised for them (2 Corinthians 5:13-15 NLT).

It's a life worth living, that's for sure. And I wish I could report to you that I've become an expert at saying yes. But I know in my heart that I'm just getting started. I'll sum it up this way, as an encouragement to you, especially if you're of the controlling, risk-adverse type, like I naturally would be apart from faith in Jesus:

> Your mission is to live for Christ. He died for you, so that your old life could die too, and He rose again in power to lay claim to your soul forever. Joining Him means you are the clay, and He is the potter. Joining Him means adventure ahead: faith, risk, love, loss, fire, trial, blessing, fun, perseverance, friends, jail, freedom, sickness, healing, riches, poverty, hard work, hope, tears, challenge . . . and at the end of all of it, however it ends, a rich welcome into the kingdom of heaven.

Your mission awaits, should you choose to accept it.

QUESTIONS FOR THOUGHT

1. Dan's mom had to choose to walk away from her comfort zone in order to say yes to God. What is your comfort zone? She also had to become transparent about a past sin in her life. What are you hiding that God might want to use for His kingdom's advancement?

2. "A *yes to God* life will lead you to places you never expected to go, with people you would never have otherwise met." Just a few examples:

   - Enoch was taken from this life so that he did not experience death.
   - Abraham was called to go to a place he would later receive as an inheritance.
   - Rahab welcomed the spies in peace and was not killed. She was given a new family!

   Where is your *yes* taking you? Who are you encountering?

3. Paul was shipwrecked, spent a night and a day in the open sea, experienced danger from bandits, and the list goes on (2 Corinthians 11:23-29). His *yes* cost him tremendously. "Whoever wants to be my disciple must deny themselves and take up their cross and follow me. For whoever wants to save their life will lose it, but whoever loses their life for me and for the gospel will save it. What good is it for someone to gain the whole world, yet forfeit their soul?" (Mark 8:34-36). What does this Scripture mean to you personally? How are you living it out in your life?

4. Do you lean toward yes or no when God speaks? Which of the following statements do you find yourself most often saying? "That will never work." "That wouldn't really happen." "I'm not ready for that." "I'd never be able to afford it."

5. Not every Christian has the same calling. Not all will be foster parents, pastors, or involved in village missions. But our calling is definitely to live the Great Commission. Read the following verse out loud: "Therefore go and make disciples of all nations, baptizing them in the name of the Father and of the Son and of the Holy Spirit, and teaching them to obey everything I have commanded you" (Matthew 28:19-20). How can pursuing this Great Commission become a bigger part of your life?

6. Insert your name into this scenario: "_____, it's so great you are here! I'm curious, Jesus commended you for being a faithful servant. What exactly did you do to be faithful to Him?"

7. What is one picture in your life's album that would never have happened apart from you saying yes?

8. Your mission is to live for Christ. He died for you so that your old life could die too; and He rose again in power to lay claim to your soul forever. Joining Him means adventure ahead: faith, risk, love, loss, fire, trial, blessing, fun, perseverance, friends, jail, freedom, sickness, healing, riches, poverty, hard work, hope, tears, challenge . . . and at the end of it, however it ends, a rich welcome into heaven. Your mission awaits. Do you choose to accept it? Is there anything holding you back?

chapter seven

YES TO GOD CHANGES EVERYTHING

John Avant

I want to be a man who walks with God. I want to live my life for God's yes.

Look at the first words of Jesus' disciples to Him in the gospel of John: "Where are you staying?" And Jesus' invitation for them: "Come . . . and you will see" (1:38-39).

I want to say yes to that invitation. Do you? Who wouldn't want to walk with the One who is perfect wisdom and perfect love?

The Bible talks about people who walked with God. Enoch was the first (Genesis 5:24), and then there was Noah (Genesis 6:9). But the Bible also says that our natural tendency is to walk away from God, not with Him: "We all, like sheep, have gone astray, each of us has turned to our own way" (Isaiah 53:6).

Maybe this is true because God doesn't always walk where we want to go, regardless of whether it is a beautiful and powerful thing to walk with God.

Saying yes to God and staying with Him day by day changes everything in our lives—as does saying no to Him.

A lot is at stake. Everything that matters, in fact.

LESSONS ON THE TRAIL OF "YES TO GOD"

I have a special place where I walk with Jesus—and sometimes with others. May I take you there in these last few pages?

The trail I am about to take you to is a very important place in my life. It's a place where I meet God in authenticity and explore His majesty. It is wild. It is arduous. It is challenging. It is a place where God speaks and where I have the choice to say yes or no.

As a child, I often walked through the Smokies with my dad. As a twenty-year-old newlywed, I walked through the Smokies with my bride on our honeymoon. As a young father, I walked through the Smokies with my son, and with all the men of our family as we camped together and sought to become men of God. My life has been forged on these trails.

In order to get there, we turn right at the "Townsend Y" and then left past the Great Smoky Mountains Institute. We drive three more miles on a rough gravel road. Along the way we see a powerful river hosting boulders the size of houses. We see breathtaking mountain vistas where I can't help but recall Psalm 121:1-2, "I lift up my eyes to the mountains—where does my help come from? My help comes from the LORD, the Maker of heaven and earth."

The gravel road comes to an end at the head of the Middle Prong trail. We make our way to the bridge where the trail begins.

Middle Prong Trail, Great Smoky National Park, Gatlinburg, TN
(Photo: Brian Stansberry / Creative Commons)

We are surrounded by wild woods and wilderness, but we are also standing where there once was a bustling city. The trail begins at the lost city of Tremont.

In 1918, William Walker sold his land, the Middle Prong watershed, to the Little River Lumber Company. Walker was the first settler in the region, having arrived there in 1859. He was a colorful character and a legendary sharpshooter. He was also a polygamist, marrying three wives and fathering twenty-six children. He loved his land and did not want it logged, but after a debilitating stroke, he had no choice but to sell. By 1925, after Walker's death, the lumber company had begun their work.

As the trees came down, the town of Tremont (meaning "Tree Mountain") rose up. Soon, right in the middle of the wilderness, there was a thriving city, with a post office, a general store, maintenance facilities for the logging equipment, a church, and a movie theater. Because of the number of families moving there, a school was eventually built. And it was in the schoolhouse that a man named Fred Cope threw the switch that brought electricity to the Smokies.

Church in Middle Prong (Courtesy Little River Railroad Museum)

With growth came the Tremont Hotel. People came from all around to stay here, especially in the summer, in the cool mountain air. Tremont was a prosperous oasis. One author who lived there called it a "crystal playground."[17]

Tremont Hotel (Courtesy Little River Railroad Museum)

But the beauty and prosperity of Tremont was short-lived. The Little River Lumber Company built a railroad in Tremont that led all the way up the mountain. It was built to transport loggers and equipment up the mountain and bring logs back down. It fulfilled its purpose very well. By 1938, the last logs had come down. The forest had been denuded, and the watershed had effectively been destroyed. The purpose of Tremont disappeared. Eventually, so did Tremont.

The people of Tremont had said yes to self-consumption until there was nothing left to consume. That danger is always before us as well.

Saying yes to self never truly satisfies. It ultimately destroys the very thing for which we yearn—a life of joy and meaning.

As I look at the remains of the railroad track, it strikes me that once this track was laid, it was easy to predict where the train would go. The train cannot turn left if the tracks turn to the right, and vice versa.

Right now, you are laying the "tracks" of your life. You will board the train and go where those tracks lead. If you keep laying the tracks the way you are now, you can easily predict where you will go.

Old railroad track (Photo: Brian Stansberry/Creative Commons)

Are you happy with that direction? What do you think is at the end? If you are not happy with the current destination, when will you begin to lay the track of your life in a different direction?

I challenge you today, following the words of Hebrews 3:13 ("Exhort one another every day, as long as it is called 'today,' that none of you may be hardened by the deceitfulness of sin" ESV), to change the direction of the tracks you will lay in the future to take you toward a new destination.

Life Lesson #1: When you say yes to God over self, He replenishes your resources, and you will never run out of all you need.

As you and I continue up the trail, we follow the path where the railroad tracks once were. We soon come to an awe-inspiring sight: Lynn Camp Falls, the longest falls in the Smokies.

Lynn Camp Falls

I invite you to consider with me the passages that have spoken to me so many times while standing before these falls. "Deep calls to deep in the roar of your waterfalls" (Psalm 42:7). As the psalmist wrote, he was longing for more of God: "As the deer pants for streams of water, so my soul pants for you, my God" (v. 1). He longed for God not out of joy but out of sorrow: "My tears have been my food day and night" (v. 3).

I wonder . . . as the last days of Tremont drew near, when there were no more trees to harvest, did anyone stand here and hear God call to them from the depth of the waterfalls to the depth of their soul? Because He will call to us. He is calling right now.

Say yes. "Yes, Lord, I will trust You even in the mysteries and sorrows of life."

After you do, God will speak again, with exactly what your soul needs.

The psalmist knew that truth from past experiences of saying yes. In verse 11 he said, "Why, my soul, are you downcast? Why so disturbed within me? Put your hope in God, for I will yet praise him, my Savior and my God."

Life Lesson #2: When you say yes to God, He speaks His yes over you.

On we go together. Another mile or so, surrounded by beauty, and we are tempted to think all may have turned out well for the city of Tremont after all. How could anyone live and work here in this beauty and *not* say yes to God? But it is not so. Other priorities called them off the path. They heard other voices.

A small, almost unnoticeable side trail appears before us to our right. We take it and walk only twenty yards or so, when a surprising and sad sight appears before us.

Rusted Cadillac

No one knows for sure the story of this 1920s Cadillac. It is thought to have possibly belonged to Colonel William Townsend himself, whom the nearby town of Townsend is named after, and the owner of the Little River Lumber Company. What we do know is that it now lies here broken and abandoned, rusted and ruined—a sad symbol of the city of Tremont.

But it does not have to symbolize your life! Not unless you choose a life of saying no to God. *Yes* transforms. *No* decays.

Life Lesson #3: When you say yes to God, you never have to be alone or stay broken.

On we go for another half mile. Before us we see a clearing and a sign in the middle of the trail. We have come to the crossroads.

Crossroads

Now we must choose. We can stay on the trail and finish our course, or we can detour.

This crossroads reminds me of the daily choice before each of us. Yes to God's voice. Yes to God's path. Or yes to the detour.

All of us detour sometimes. We will wander away. But God pursues us in love. He calls us back to Himself. And He will always give us the grace to say yes and to walk His trail with Him again.

Life Lesson #4: Saying yes to God is the most important decision you will make every day of your life.

At the three-mile mark, we see a haunting scene just off to our left. To me it is the saddest part of our journey.

As far as I know, what we see is the only remaining part of any building standing from the lost city of Tremont. It was someone's home. The fire from the fireplace warmed a family. When I first made this hike, the entire chimney was still standing after almost one hundred years. But by my next hike, it had crumbled and fallen, bringing to mind this truth: "Unless the LORD builds the house, the builders labor in vain" (Psalm 127:1).

Ruined house

I know nothing about the residents of this fallen house. But I do know something about another building that has disappeared: the Tremont Hotel.

As the city of Tremont grew, something began to happen that changed the nature of the town from a place of beauty and prosperity to a place of darkness and degradation . . . from a place where people came to experience the wonder of God's creation, to a place parents warned their children to avoid. The Tremont Hotel became a house of ill repute. It was known as "the Sodom and Gomorrah of its day."[18]

The Bible records in Genesis 19 what happened to Sodom and Gomorrah. Now all the houses and buildings of Tremont are like this one ruin along our trail—wrecked, abandoned, and forgotten. Tremont exists no longer because the people of the city said yes to self and no to God. They did it while there was a functioning church right in their midst.

Nothing is stopping us right now from saying no to self— no to every other voice—and saying yes to God.

Life Lesson #5: The future of your life, family, and church will be determined by your yes to God.

We could go farther along this trail, but it's time for us to start our journey back. God is calling us. Can you hear Him? He beckons us to journey with Him to wonderful places.

As we walk the three miles back, there is no sign that this forest was once completely destroyed. The trees once again stand tall, restored like a healing miracle of God. It's an easy walk back, because the trail is now downhill. And all along the way, we are surrounded by God's beauty.

As we leave the lost city of Tremont behind us, we head back to our daily journey with these five lessons to guide us. But more than that, we have a King who is with us. A King who will heal us just like He did this forest.

And He speaks! So each one of us who knows Him as Savior and Friend has the privilege of hearing Him and saying yes. Say yes to this life! Say yes to this God! Why would we ever do otherwise?

Paul ended his letter to the Ephesians with these words:

Now to him who is able to do immeasurably more than all we ask or imagine, according to his power that is at work within us, to him be glory in the church and in Christ Jesus throughout all generations, for ever and ever! Amen (Ephesians 3:20-21).

By the way, the last word of that passage is *Amen*. And *Amen* means YES!

QUESTIONS FOR THOUGHT

1. When you say yes to God over self, He replenishes your resources, and you will never run out of all you need. What do these words mean to you?

   - "I lift up my eyes to the mountains—where does my help come from? My help comes from the LORD, the Maker of heaven and earth" (Psalm 121:1-2).

   - "My God will meet all your needs according to the riches of his glory in Christ Jesus" (Philippians 4:19).

   Tell God what it is you need right now. Believe His promises.

2. When you say yes to God, even when life is hard, He speaks His yes over you. What is difficult in your life right now? Read the following Scriptures, knowing that He is speaking them over you.

   - "Why, my soul, are you downcast? Why so disturbed within me? Put your hope in God, for I will yet praise him, my Savior and my God" (Psalm 42:11).

- "The LORD your God is with you, the Mighty Warrior who saves. He will take great delight in you; in his love he will no longer rebuke you, but will rejoice over you with singing" (Zephaniah 3:17).

3. When you say yes to God, you never have to feel lonely or beyond hope. Are you despairing? Express that to God. Read His Word out loud and believe His promises.

   - "Do not conform to the pattern of this world, but be transformed by the renewing of your mind. Then you will be able to test and approve what God's will is—his good, pleasing and perfect will" (Romans 12:2).

   - "Be strong and courageous. Do not be afraid or terrified because of them, for the LORD your God goes with you; he will never leave you nor forsake you" (Deuteronomy 31:6).

4. Saying yes to God is the single most important decision you will make every day of your life. Are you doubting this truth? Be honest. What does God's Word say?

   - "See, I set before you today life and prosperity, death and destruction. For I command you today to love the LORD your God, to walk in obedience to him, and to keep his commands . . . and the LORD your God will bless you in the land you are entering to possess" (Deuteronomy 30:15-16).

   - "Seek first his kingdom and his righteousness, and all these things will be given to you as well" (Matthew 6:33).

5. The future of your life, family, and church will be determined by your yes to God. What do you want your future to look like? What is the future of your family? What is the future of your church?

- "Unless the LORD builds the house, the builders labor in vain" (Psalm 127:1).

- "Now choose life, so that you and your children may live and that you may love the LORD your God, listen to his voice, and hold fast to him" (Deuteronomy 30:19-20).

6. Ephesians 3:20-21 says, "Now to him who is able to do immeasurably more than all we ask or imagine, according to his power that is at work within us, to him be glory in the church and in Christ Jesus throughout all generations, for ever and ever! **Amen**." To what extent do these words describe your life, your family, your church? Are you ready for God to say **amen** over your life?

ENDNOTES

1 Matt Brown, "Don't Say God Is Silent with Your Bible Closed," article on DesiringGod.org.

2 "To Hear the First Stars in the Universe, Astronomers Had to Find the Quietest Place on Earth," www.newsweek.com/hear-first-stars-universe-astronomers-quietest-place-earth-824691.

3 Paul Avant, *Jesus Speaks*, 3.

4 Ibid., 220.

5 *Hearing God's Voice*, copyright © 2002 by Henry T. Blackaby and Richard Blackaby (B&H Publishing Group: Nashville), 53.

6 *Thayer's Expanded Greek Definitions*, Electronic Database, Biblesoft, Inc., 2011.

7 "Millennials at Church: What Millennials Want When They Visit Church," *Making Space for Millennials*, Barna Group, March 4, 2015.

8 *The Complete Idiot's Guide to Learning Yiddish*, copyright © 2000 by Rabbi Benjamin Blech (Alpha Books), 48.

9 This is a paraphrase.

10 *Suffering Is Never for Nothing*, copyright © 2019 by Elisabeth Elliot Gren (B&H Publishing Group: Nashville), 9.

11 Ibid., 104.

12 Ibid., 71.

13 *New York Times*, February 18, 2018.

14 www.cigna.com/newsroom/news-releases/2018/new-cigna-study-reveals-loneliness-at-epidemic-levels-in-america

15 See Judges 6:36-40.

16 "Yes, Lord, Yes," lyrics written by Shirley Caesar.

17 Florence Cope Bush, *Dorie: Woman of the Mountains* (Knoxville: University of Tennessee Press, 1992), 171.

18 Ibid., 199.

ABOUT THE AUTHORS

John and Donna met and completed their undergraduate degrees at Baylor University in Waco, Texas. John went on to earn a Masters of Divinity and a Ph.D. from Southwestern Baptist Theological Seminary in Fort Worth. It was at Southwestern that John learned about spiritual awakening and revival. He believes our nation's only hope is to experience a mighty movement of God.

From the moment they met, John and Donna shared a call to ministry. John has pastored in Texas, Louisiana, Georgia, and Tennessee. While he was pastoring Coggin Avenue Baptist Church in Brownwood, Texas, the Lord began a revival that spread to over one hundred college campuses, including Wheaton College. John also served as Vice President of Evangelism and Spiritual Awakening at the North American Mission Board. Donna has always served alongside him by teaching and mentoring women.

John and Donna have had the privilege of sharing the love of Christ and supporting missionaries all over the world. They have a passion to see the recent, unprecedented move of God that many overseas countries are experiencing come to America.

John serves as President of *Life Action*, inspiring people to say yes to God. He has authored five books: *Revival*; *The Passion Promise*; *Authentic Power*; *If God Were Real*; and *Revival Revived*. Donna has authored *No Excuses*, a Bible study of 1 and 2 Timothy, and is a contributing author to *A Daily Women's Devotional* and *Revive* magazine. They live in Knoxville, Tennessee, and have three married children and six grandchildren. On a day off, you are likely to find them hiking the Smoky Mountains or swimming with their grandchildren. Or you might find John scuba diving or playing golf.

We inspire your next **YES** to God.

Over the past 50 years in thousands of locations, *Life Action* has been inspiring millions of people to say yes to God's vision for life—yes to love, yes to faith, yes to revival, yes to transformation.

Your next yes could be just around the corner, and who knows where it might lead?

EXPERIENCE LIFE ACTION THROUGH:

Media　　　Church Events　　　Camps and Retreats

LifeAction.org

Ready for the ultimate family vacation?

If you are looking for a fun-filled, family-centered vacation, discover *Life Action*'s Family Camp. You'll experience **passionate** and **biblical** teaching, **vibrant** worship, and a host of **exciting** activities all designed for your entire family.

Learn more about Family Camp and other retreats at
LifeActionCamp.com

LIFE-CHANGING EVENTS *FOR YOUR ENTIRE CHURCH*

LifeAction.org/Church-Events

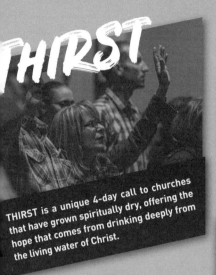

THIRST is a unique 4-day call to churches that have grown spiritually dry, offering the hope that comes from drinking deeply from the living water of Christ.

Life Action's Revive Conference offers smaller and mid-sized churches a Bible-centered, personal application-focused experience with one of *Life Action's* speakers.

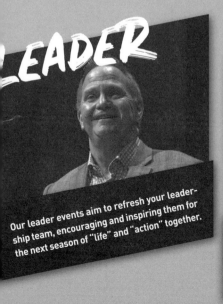

Our leader events aim to refresh your leadership team, encouraging and inspiring them for the next season of "life" and "action" together.

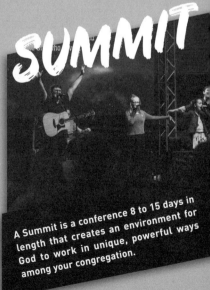

A Summit is a conference 8 to 15 days in length that creates an environment for God to work in unique, powerful ways among your congregation.

YES CHANGES
[Insert Your Group Here]

Your group, class, or church family can
jump into the yes life by downloading
additional resources related to this
book, including videos by authors
John and Donna Avant.

ACCESS THE YES CHANGES EVERYTHING
TEACHING SERIES ONLINE:

LifeAction.org/YesChangesEverything